The Future Impact of Automation on Workers

The Future Impact of Automation on Workers

Wassily Leontief
Faye Duchin

New York Oxford
Oxford University Press
1986

Oxford University Press

Oxford   New York   Toronto
Delhi   Bombay   Calcutta   Madras   Karachi
Petaling Jaya   Singapore   Hong Kong   Tokyo
Nairobi   Dar es Salaam   Cape Town
Melbourne   Auckland

and associated companies in
Beirut   Berlin   Ibadan   Nicosia

Library of Congress Catologing in Publication Data

Leontief, Wassily W.
The future impact of automation on workers.
Includes index.
1. Labor supply—United States—Effect of technological
innovations on—Mathematical models.   2. Employment
forecasting—United States—Mathematical models.
3. Input-output tables—United States.   I. Duchin,
Faye.   II. Title.
HD5724.L38   1985   331.1   85-3082
ISBN 0-19-503623-9

Printing (last digit):   9 8 7 6 5 4 3 2 1

Printed in the United States of America

Preface

The analysis presented in this book addresses the complex issues surrounding the impact of computer-based automation on employment in the United States in the recent past and, especially, through the end of the century. At the same time that the computer revolution has created hundreds of thousands of new jobs, it has threatened hundreds of thousands of other jobs with obsolescence. Behind this shift is the economic pressure to improve productivity, and part of the price of productivity improvement will be the displacement of workers by computer-based machines.

The impact of automation on the future course of employment is a subject that merits the best thinking and research that can be brought to it. The findings reported in this book represent the preliminary, thought-provoking outcome of an ambitious effort to develop and apply systematic procedures to the analysis of various aspects of the structural transformation of the U.S. economy. We use the input-output approach in this analysis, a method that has been widely applied to examining structural economic change in the United States and many other countries. In this application, we have combined a new computer-based mathematical model with a large database assembled in large part "by hand" from many sources.

After a general discussion of the impact of automation on employment, we analyze how automation is likely to affect employment in four specific areas of the economy: manufacturing sectors, office work, education, and health care. The input-output approach makes it possible to draw conclusions regarding both overall employment and the prospects for individual occupations—all fully integrated into a broader economic description that provides the context for evaluating their significance.

The book is likely to be stimulating and useful for a wide range of readers concerned about the future implications of automation. Those who have some familiarity with the emerging computer-based technologies and with at least simple quantitative methods should have no difficulty following the discussion. Experts will also find the material informative, especially since the procedures incorporate initiatives not previously found in this type of work.

The research on which this book is based involved the efforts of many of the authors' colleagues at the Institute for Economic Analysis. Dr. Daniel Szyld collaborated in the development of the mathematical model and supervised the computations and assembly of the database.

Several researchers compiled the data about the future use of computer-based automation. Dr. David Howell's work on computers, robots, and machine tools is reported in Chapter 2. Chapter 3 on office automation was prepared and drafted by Catherine McDonough, and Chapters 4 through 6 on education, health care, and public and private consumption are based on the work of Glenn-Marie Lange. The historical data were assembled by Jesus Alvarez and Michel Juillard and are described in Appendix B.

Dimitri Turchin was responsible for implementing and maintaining the database and computer model and was assisted in computations at different periods by Kenneth Furlong, Vladimir Roytman, and Oleg Vishnepolsky.

This book is based on research supported by the National Science Foundation under contract #PRA-8012844. Any opinions, findings, conclusions, or recommendations expressed in this publication are those of the authors and do not necessarily reflect the views of the National Science Foundation.

New York   W. L.
January 1985   F. D.

Contents

List of Abbreviations

BEA	Bureau of Economic Analysis
BLS	Bureau of Labor Statistics
CBI	Computer-Based Instruction
CFT	Capital Flow Table
E&D	Eating and Drinking Places
IEA	Institute for Economic Analysis
IEA #nn	Sector number nn in the IEA sectoral classification scheme
IO	Input-output
ITV	Instructional Television
LAB #mm	Occupation number mm in the IEA occupation classification scheme
na	not available
NC (CNC)	Numerically Controlled (Computer-Numerically-Controlled)
nec	not elsewhere classified
NIPA	National Income and Product Accounts
OA	Office Automation
SIC	Standard Industrial Classification

List of Tables

List of Figures

The Future Impact of Automation on Workers

CHAPTER 1

The Future Impact of Automation on Employment

Opinions about automation expressed in the scholarly literature as well as the popular press cover a wide range—from reassurance that declining rates of growth of the labor force in the 1980s and 1990s will more than compensate for any loss of jobs, to predictions that the manufacturing labor force will fall from currently over 25 million to less than 3 million by 2010. We are told that some jobs will become more technical and complex than ever while the "de-skilled" work force of sweepers and button-pushers grows. Most observers agree about painful "adjustment" and the needs of retraining, often in the context of measures to ease the "transition" to some automated future which remains entirely unspecified.

Barely beneath the surface of these debates, there are passionate social, political, and philosophical differences. An additional cause of confusion is that we cannot carry out a "factual" analysis, if that means direct observation, of the future. In this book, we develop and illustrate a fact-finding and modeling approach that promises to be fruitful in the dispassionate analysis of these issues. After ascertaining the operating characteristics of the already existing, newly developed types of computers and computer-based equipment, we proceed to derive the consequences of alternative assumptions concerning future rates of introduction of this equipment into the different industries. Taking into account the corresponding changes in the combination of other inputs, particularly labor inputs, we insert the appropriate figures (combinations of so-called technical input coefficients) into a dynamic input-output model and use it to trace the direct and indirect effects of these technical changes on the future levels of output and input—particularly labor inputs—throughout all sectors of the economy.

While there is no shortage of "expert" estimates of isolated numbers (like the sales of computers in 1990), the specialized literature in this area is still very limited, and robotics seems to be the only aspect

3

of automation that has been studied at all systematically to date. Technical studies like those that have so far been carried out only for robotics must be welcomed and encouraged, and their detailed findings need to be incorporated with the results of other similar studies into a comprehensive analytical framework so that useful general conclusions can be drawn. It is precisely such an effort, based on a dynamic input-output model of the U.S. economy, that is described in this book.

In the dynamic input-output model we use, the entire economy is divided into almost 100 industries producing goods and services and several consuming sectors including households and government. The model represents the detailed input requirements of each industry or sector and the interrelationships among all parts of the economy for each year between 1963 and 2000. It also links the sales in one year of the industries producing the full spectrum of capital goods with the subsequent production capacities of the sectors which purchase this plant and equipment. A more complete description of this model is found in Appendix A.

A number of other studies of structural change have been carried out within the input-output framework, starting with Wassily Leontief's analysis in the 1930s of the changing U.S. economy between 1919 and 1929 (Leontief, 1941). Most other empirical work has also been concerned with analysis of the past (Carter, 1970; Vaccara and Simon, 1968; Bezdek and Wendling, 1976). The formulation of detailed scenarios[1] to analyze future prospects was also initiated by Leontief (Leontief, Carter, and Petri, 1977). A recent input-output study of the impacts of future technological change on the Austrian economy involving construction of alternative scenarios follows in this tradition (Osterreichisches Institut, 1981). The Economic Growth Model of the Bureau of Labor Statistics (BLS) uses an input-output module within an econometric framework to project future employment (U.S. Department of Labor, 1982b). We have made extensive use of the historical data prepared by this group, directed by Ronald Kutscher, in the development of our model. We have also used their detailed projections of final demand.

Alternative technological scenarios are formulated and computed within the framework of the dynamic input-output model of the U.S.

---

1. "Scenario," in the narrow sense, means a set of assumptions about certain aspects of the economy. When the implications of the scenario are computed, projections of other aspects of the economy are obtained. The word is also used to mean the projections implied by the assumptions.

economy developed for this study. This means that intertemporal consistency is assured between the production of investment goods and their subsequent availability. The level and composition of each sector's annual replacement and expansion investment reflect within the framework of this model the particular technological and growth conditions postulated in each scenario.[2] The data work carried out for this study, although still very far from exhaustive, is more comprehensive and more fully documented than that used in most other descriptions of the U.S. economy, especially with regard to future technological options, and the alternative scenarios are designed so as to focus attention on intensive examination of the changing structure of employment.

It needs to be emphasized at the outset that this study represents only a first step in anticipating the future demand for labor. In addition to the preliminary nature of the work that has been done, we have concentrated on only one—albeit the newest, most talked about—component of technological change: computer-based automation. Our most substantial results will be based on the comparison of employment projections under alternative assumptions about computer-based automation. While some readers may be tempted to draw more general conclusions about future technological unemployment, such an analysis cannot be supported by the work which has been done to date.

The first chapter of this book provides an overview of the study and reports the results. The remaining five chapters contain sector studies on the automation of production and office operations, education, and health care which serve as the basis for the alternative scenarios about the future. Appendix A contains a relatively nontechnical description of a simple input-output model followed by a more technical description of the model that was developed for, and first used in, this study. The historical data used in the analysis are described in Appendix B.

Methodology and Scenarios

To improve the understanding of the impacts of past technological change on employment in the U.S. and to assess the probable effects of impending computer-based automation on the demand for labor over the next few decades, a dynamic input-output model of the U.S. econ-

---

2. The World Model (Leontief, Carter, and Petri, 1977) took some steps in these directions: all the other cited studies were carried out essentially within a comparative static framework.

omy was developed and an extensive database was prepared containing descriptions of past and present technologies and of technological changes to be introduced in the relatively near future. Four different scenarios were formulated, and alternative projections based on them were computed with the model to determine the structure of employment corresponding to each of them. This section provides an overview of the methodology and describes the scenarios. Formal descriptions of the model and the data used in its practical implementation are provided in the following chapters and in the appendices.

The national economy consists of a set of interrelated sectors each characterized at a given time by a common principal output and the combination of inputs required to produce that output—including labor inputs of various types. The establishments in each sector employ in any given year a specific mix of machines, tools, and human labor to transform a specific combination of purchased inputs (produced by the same or other sectors) into the characteristic output of the sector.

At any given time there are typically several distinct technologies or production processes in use at different establishments within a sector or even at a single plant. The average combination of inputs that characterize the sector corresponds to both the input requirements of alternative technologies and the weight with which each alternative operates in the national economy. Technological change involves a change in these weights, in which typically the newest technologies are progressively phased in (increased weight) and the oldest eliminated (decreased weight). Of course, technological change also involves the introduction of new processes and products that were not previously available.

Portions of a sector's stock of plant and equipment are periodically replaced, while current additions to it make possible an increase of output in the future. The technological requirements for the replacement of existing capital (i.e., to maintain current production capacity) are in large part dictated by the mix of investment goods already in place and to this extent reflect the technologies already in use. Some modernization also takes place; this involves the incorporation of newly available technologies into existing plants. However, in a growing economy the new technologies are typically reflected first in newly produced capital equipment installed expressly for the expansion of existing capacity—and naturally in the occupational composition of the labor force which works with the physical capital and other inputs.

The state of the national economy in each year over the time interval 1963–2000 is described in terms of commodity flows among 89 producing sectors and labor inputs absorbed by each of them specified in terms of 53 occupations. Numerical data are organized for each year into four matrices of technical parameters describing the input structures of all sectors of the economy during that year. These matrices specify the input requirements on current account (A matrix), capital expansion and replacement requirements (B and R matrices, respectively), and labor inputs (L matrix) of each sector per unit of its respective total output—or per unit of projected future increase in capacity in the case of expansion. Vectors of noninvestment final demand, including household consumption, government purchases, and net exports (y vector) are also required. The mathematical model representing the relationships among these matrices and vectors is described in nontechnical terms in Appendix A. For the past years, government agencies produced official series containing most of this information: the sources and data preparation are described in Appendix B.

Figures describing future technological options are assembled as part of separate sector studies which appear in Chapters 2–6. These sector studies yielded descriptions of alternative input structures (i.e., columns and rows of technical coefficients that are inserted into the A, B, R, and L matrices). They also yielded projected vectors of noninvestment final demand (y) for future years. The fact-finding efforts were concentrated on the systematic study of computers used to automate production and office operations as well as the potential for automation in the education and health-care sectors. Table 1.1 indicates the rows and columns of coefficients, including capital and labor coefficients, which have been reexamined.

In addition to this database, the structure of the model can be seen as reflecting explicit conceptual assumptions about how the economy works, independent of the specific values assigned to different variables and parameters. The structure of the model implicitly determines the range of questions that can be examined, and the dynamic input-output model used in this analysis makes it possible to begin to answer questions—like those analyzed in this study—that could not formerly be concretely addressed.

The dynamic input-output model is used to project, year by year from 1963 to 2000, the sectoral outputs and investment and labor requirements of the U.S. economy under alternative assumptions about its changing technological structure. Each set of such assumptions constitutes a scenario.

Four different scenarios (S1, S2, S3, and S4), tracing four alternative paths that the U.S. economy might follow between 1980 and 2000,

TABLE 1.1. Location of the 1980 Technical Coefficients Re-Examined for Projections to 1990 and 2000[a,b]

IEA #	Sector		1	2	3	4	5	6	7	8	9	10	11	12	13	14	15	16	17	18	19	20	21	22	23	24	25	26	27	28	29	30	31	32
																		A, B, and R Matrices																
1–4	Agriculture	1																	x	x	x	x		x								x	x	
5–10	Mining	2																	x	x	x	x		x								x	x	x
11	Construction	3																	x	x	x	x		x								x	x	
12	Ordnance	4																	x	x	x	x										x	x	
13, 14	Food, etc.	5																	x	x	x	x		x								x	x	
15–18, 32, 33	Textiles, etc.	6																	x	x	x	x		x								x	x	
19–25	Lumber, Paper, etc.	7																	x	x	x	x		x								x	x	
26–28, 31	Chemicals, etc.	8																	x	x	x	x		x								x	x	
29	Paints	9				x	x	x	x	x	x	x							x	x	x	x	x	x	x	x						x	x	
30	Petroleum Refining	10																	x	x	x	x		x								x	x	
34, 35	Glass, Stone, Clay	11																	x	x	x	x	x									x	x	
36	Iron and Steel	12			x	x	x	x	x	x	x	x	x	x					x	x	x	x	x		x							x	x	
37	Nonferrous Metals	13																	x	x	x	x	x									x	x	
38–41	Metal Products	14																	x	x	x	x		x								x	x	
46	Metal Working Machinery	15				x	x	x	x	x	x	x	x	x	x	x	x	x	x	x	x	x		x		x						x	x	
42–45, 47–49, 52	Other Machinery	16																	x	x	x	x		x	x	x						x		
86	Robots	17		x	x	x	x	x	x	x	x	x	x	x	x	x	x		x	x	x	x	x	x	x	x	x	x	x	x	x		x	x
50	Computers	18		x	x	x	x	x	x	x	x	x	x	x	x	x	x		x	x	x	x	x	x	x	x	x	x	x	x	x	x	x	x
51	Office Equipment	19		x	x	x	x	x	x	x	x	x	x	x	x				x	x	x	x	x		x	x	x	x	x	x	x			
53–55, 60	Electrical Equip., etc.	20																	x	x	x	x	x									x	x	
56	Communications Equip.	21																	x	x	x	x		x								x	x	
57–59	Electronic Components	22																	x	x	x	x	x	x		x	x	x	x	x	x	x		
61–63	Transportation Equip.	23																	x	x	x	x		x								x	x	
64–66	Other Manufacturing	24																	x	x	x	x		x								x	x	
67, 71, 72	Transp. and Trade	25																	x	x	x	x	x									x	x	
68, 69	Communications	26																	x	x	x	x	x									x	x	
70	Utilities	27																	x	x	x	x		x								x	x	
73–75	Fin., Insur., and R.E.	28																	x	x	x	x		x		x	x	x	x	x	x	x	x	
77	Business Services	29																	x	x	x	x		x								x	x	
81, 82	Health Care	30																	x	x	x	x		x								x	x	
83, 87–89	Education	31																	x	x	x	x	x			x	x	x	x	x	x	x	x	
76, 78–80, 84, 85	Other Services	32																	x	x	x	x		x		x	x	x	x	x	x	x	x	x

L Matrices

LAB #	Occupation		1	2	3	4	5	6	7	8	9	10	11	12	13	14	15	16	17	18	19	20	21	22	23	24	25	26	27	28	29	30	31	32
1–5	Eng. and Sci. (1.5%)[c]	1		x	x		x	x	x	x	x	x	x	x	x	x	x	x	x	x	x	x	x	x	x	x	x	x	x	x	x	x	x	x
6–8	Computer Prof. (0.4)	2		x	x	x	x	x	x	x	x	x	x	x	x	x	x	x	x	x	x	x	x	x	x	x	x	x	x	x	x	x	x	
10–13	Health Prof. (2.7)	3																														x		
14	Teachers (4.5)	4																															x	
15	Drafters (0.3)	5		x	x		x	x	x	x	x	x	x	x	x	x	x	x	x	x	x	x	x	x	x	x	x	x	x	x				
9, 16	Other Prof. (6.0)	6		x	x	x	x	x	x	x	x	x	x	x	x	x	x	x	x	x	x	x	x	x	x	x	x	x	x	x	x	x	x	
17	Managers (10.6)	7	x	x	x	x	x	x	x	x	x	x	x	x	x	x	x	x	x	x	x	x	x	x	x	x	x	x	x	x	x	x	x	
18	Sales Workers (6.6)	8		x	x	x	x	x	x	x	x	x	x	x	x	x	x	x	x	x	x	x	x	x	x	x	x	x	x		x	x	x	
19–24	Clerical (17.8)	9	x	x	x	x	x	x	x	x	x	x	x	x	x	x	x	x	x	x	x	x	x	x	x	x	x	x	x	x	x	x	x	
25–28	Constr. Crafts. (3.8)	10		x	x		x	x	x	x	x	x	x	x	x	x	x	x	x	x	x	x	x	x	x	x	x	x				x		
30–32	Metalw. Crafts. (1.3)	11		x	x		x	x	x	x	x	x	x	x	x	x	x	x	x	x	x	x	x	x	x	x	x	x						
47	Robot. Technicians (—)	12					x	x	x	x	x	x	x	x	x	x	x	x	x	x	x	x	x	x	x	x								
33	Mechanics (3.9)	13		x	x		x	x	x	x	x	x	x	x	x	x	x	x	x	x	x	x	x	x	x	x	x	x				x		
34–38	Other Craftsmen (4.3)	14		x	x		x	x	x	x	x	x	x	x	x	x	x	x	x	x	x	x	x	x	x	x	x	x				x		
39	Assemblers (1.2)	15															x	x	x	x	x	x	x	x	x	x								
40	Inspectors (0.8)	16															x	x	x	x	x	x	x	x	x	x								
41	Packers (0.8)	17															x	x	x	x	x	x	x	x	x	x								
42	Painters (0.2)	18															x	x	x	x	x	x	x	x	x									
43	Welders (0.7)	19															x	x	x	x	x	x	x	x	x									
44–45	Delivery Workers (2.6)	20					x	x	x	x	x	x	x	x	x	x	x	x	x	x	x	x	x	x	x	x	x	x				x		
46	Other Operatives (9.4)	21		x	x		x	x	x	x	x	x	x	x	x	x	x	x	x	x	x	x	x	x	x	x	x	x				x		
48	Janitors (1.5)	22																	x	x				x	x							x		
50	Food Svc. Work. (3.9)	23																	x	x				x	x									
49, 51	Other Svc. Work. (6.9)	24																	x	x				x		x						x		
52	Laborers (4.9)	25		x	x		x	x	x	x	x	x	x	x	x	x	x	x	x	x	x	x	x	x	x	x	x	x				x	x	
53	Farm Workers (3.2)	26																														x	x	

aThe first matrix in this figure has 32 rows and 32 columns, corresponding to 32 sectors of the economy. The second matrix has 26 rows and 32 columns, corresponding to 26 occupations and the same 32 sectors as the first matrix. These sectoral and occupational classification schemes are more aggregated than those used in the IEA model. The correspondence is given by the codes in the columns preceding the sector and occupation names in the figure, labeled IEA # and LAB #, respectively. These codes, in turn, are described in Tables B.1 and B.9.

bThe letter 'x' indicates an entry that has been explicitly projected for this study; 'x' may represent a zero; e.g., a full column of x's does not necessarily mean that the sector purchases all inputs. 'x' does not necessarily mean that the entry projected for a future year is different from the base-year value (although this is typically the case). For example, the column representing Office Equipment is filled with x's because the future input structure of that sector was explicitly examined; however, in the A matrix only a single entry in that column is expected to change significantly from the base year value. Many empty cells contain zeros. For example, the rows for Health Professionals and Teachers each contain only 1 'x' because these workers are virtually all employed by the Health Care and Education sectors, respectively.

cNumber in parentheses shows corresponding percentage of 1978 labor force.

were formulated and computed. These were selected with the view of bracketing among them the upper and the lower limits of the rates at which different sectors of the U.S. economy might be expected to adopt the new technology. The *reference scenario*, S1, represents the changing input-output structure of the economy, year by year, between 1963 and 1980, but assumes no further automation or any other technological change after 1980. In other words, from 1980 on, robots, numerically controlled machine tools, and automated office equipment—to name a few examples—are used only to the extent that they figured in the average technologies that prevailed in 1980. Final demand, comprising private household consumption, government consumption, and net exports, however, is assumed to continue to grow over a projected path through 2000. The computation of this scenario is thus an experiment that allows us to assess future employment and other requirements to satisfy plausible final demand in the absence of technological improvements from 1980 on: it serves as a baseline with which one can compare the other scenarios.

Scenarios S2 and S3 are identical with S1 through 1980 but differ in their technological assumptions for the later years. Both scenarios project an increasing use of computers in all sectors for specific information processing and machine control tasks and their integration. Computerizing each task also involves changes in other inputs, notably labor inputs. While the details are different in each case, Scenario S3 assumes faster technological progress and the more rapid adoption of available technologies than does S2; for example, the availability of more powerful software to dampen the demand for programmers and more rapid elimination of human drafters. Under both scenarios, the demand for computers (measured in constant prices per unit of output) is naturally higher in 2000 than in 1990.

These scenarios also represent the greater use of robots and computer-numerically-controlled (CNC) machine tools for a growing range of specific manufacturing operations. Scenario S3 assumes a faster replacement by robots for six categories of production workers in many manufacturing sectors. It also involves faster substitution than S2 of CNC for conventional machine tools and greater savings per tool in steel scrap, leading to corresponding reductions in direct requirements for the metalworking occupations.

All projections assume that computer-based workstations will be replacing conventional office equipment, and that most deliveries after 1985 will be for integrated electronic systems rather than stand-alone devices. The process is accelerated under Scenario S3 where, for example, conventional typewriters are no longer produced after 1985. Corresponding direct impacts on the demand for managerial, sales, and six categories of clerical workers in different sectors of the economy are represented in detail.

Both Scenarios S2 and S3 assume the continuation of recent trends in the input structures of the health-care sectors, notably the increased use per case of various types of capital equipment for diagnosis and treatment, of drugs and other chemicals, and of plastic disposable items, as well as an expansion of nonphysician medical personnel. These changes proceed more rapidly under Scenario S3 than S2. The health-care sectors also continue the automation of office-type operations, with the direct consequences described above. Under Scenario S1, there are no structural changes, in these or other sectors, after 1980.

Just as computers are increasingly affecting the conduct of professional and leisure activities, the demand for computer-based education, training, recreation in schools, on the job, and in homes will also increase. In all years through 2000 Scenario S3 assumes far more computer-based courses per student and more teacher training than Scenario S2. It also postulates on-the-job training in more sectors and for a greater number of occupations.

The dynamic input-output model used in this study requires that projections of final demand other than investment—essentially the level and composition of future public and private consumption—be provided from outside the model. For present purposes the same BLS final demand projections (excluding deliveries for investment purposes) were used in Scenarios S1, S2, and S3 so that differences in scenario outcomes have to be attributed exclusively to the different technological assumptions.

We have not yet examined in detail the implications of technological and demographic change for the future input structures of households, of technological change and alternative government policy for the input structures of the various federal, state, and local public administration functions, or of technological change and related shifts in international comparative advantage for the composition of U.S. exports and imports. Under these circumstances we decided that the best starting point would be the BLS final demand projections which, however, have been revised upwards with respect to the use of computers by the military and by households.

Scenario S4 is identical to S3 in all of its assumptions about the technological structure of the economy, but the final demand projections incorporated into it are different from those used in the other scenarios. The reasons for this are discussed in subsequent sections.

Employment figures shown in this study do not, unless otherwise noted, include either government employees in the armed forces and in public administration positions or household workers, and the value of final deliveries does not include payments to them.

The following section describes the future demand for labor based on comparisons of alternative projections from Scenarios S1 through S4. The results of the computations show that in comparing two scenarios, many variables will be generally, but not always, higher under one than the other. A systematic difference is often not observed in every year because each scenario involves a distinct pattern of capacity utilization and investment which in turn requires distinct cyclical patterns of production, especially for capital-producing sectors. A preliminary investigation suggests that the cycles of sectoral output and of gross sectoral investment produced by this model for the period 1963–1981 bear a respectable resemblance to those that have been actually experienced. (Actual output and investment figures have not been built in to the results through a "calibration" procedure.) Nonetheless, careful analysis of the cycles will require a separate study,[3] and here we concentrate instead on the secular trends. Thus, while the tables appearing in the remainder of this chapter contain data for individual years, more than a single year is always shown and only relationships of persistent trends are illustrated.

Principal Findings

The results of this study show that the intensive use of automation will make it possible to achieve over the next 20 years significant economies in labor relative to the production of the same bills of goods with the mix of technologies currently in use. Over 11 million fewer workers are required in 1990, and over 20 million fewer in 2000, under Scenario S3 compared to S1; this represents a saving of 8.5 and 11.7%, respectively, of the reference scenario labor requirements.

The levels and composition of employment in 1978 under Scenarios S1, S2, and S3 are shown in Tables 1.2 and 1.3. BLS estimates for the same year are included for comparison. Since the same BLS sectoral

---

3. This analysis is currently in progress.

TABLE 1.2. Levels of Employment[a] Under Scenarios S1, S2, and S3 in 1978, 1990, and 2000 (Millions of Person-Years)

	Scenarios S1, S2, and S3	BLS estimates[b]
1978		
Professionals	13.9	13.3
Managers	9.5	9.6
Sales Workers	5.9	5.9
Clerical Workers	15.9	15.6
Craftsmen	11.8	12.0
Operatives	14.0	14.3
Service Workers	11.1	10.6
Laborers	4.3	4.5
Farmers	2.8	2.8
Total	89.2	88.6

	Scenario S1	Scenario S2	Scenario S3
1990			
Professionals	19.8	21.2	20.9
Managers	14.4	14.4	12.4
Sales Workers	9.1	8.9	8.2
Clerical Workers	24.7	21.2	16.7
Craftsmen	18.0	17.9	17.5
Operatives	22.0	21.8	21.1
Service Workers	16.7	16.8	16.8
Laborers	6.6	6.6	6.4
Farmers	4.2	4.2	4.2
Total	135.5	132.9	124.1
2000			
Professionals	25.6	28.4	31.1
Managers	19.0	17.1	11.2
Sales Workers	12.4	11.8	10.2
Clerical Workers	32.6	25.0	17.9
Craftsmen	23.3	22.9	23.4
Operatives	27.6	26.1	25.8
Service Workers	22.3	22.4	23.0
Laborers	8.7	8.6	8.7
Farmers	5.3	5.3	5.4
Total	176.8	167.7	156.6

[a]Includes all private sector employment (jobs) plus employment in public education and health. Does not include public administration, armed forces, or household employees.

[b]Calculated from U.S. Department of Labor (1981) using the employment definitions of the IEA Model.

13

TABLE 1.3. Composition of Employment[a] Under Scenarios S1, S2, and S3 in 1978, 1990, and 2000

	Scenarios S1, S2, and S3	BLS estimates[b]
1978		
Professionals	15.6%	15.0%
Managers	9.5	10.8
Sales Workers	6.6	6.7
Clerical Workers	17.8	17.7
Craftsmen	13.3	13.6
Operatives	15.7	16.1
Service Workers	12.4	12.0
Laborers	4.9	5.0
Farmers	3.2	3.2
Total	100.0%	100.0%

	Scenario S1	Scenario S2	Scenario S3
1990			
Professionals	14.6%	16.0%	16.8%
Managers	10.6	10.8	10.0
Sales Workers	6.7	6.7	6.6
Clerical Workers	18.2	15.9	13.5
Craftsmen	13.3	13.5	14.1
Operatives	16.3	16.4	17.0
Service Workers	12.3	12.6	13.5
Laborers	4.9	4.9	5.2
Farmers	3.1	3.1	3.3
Total	100.0%	100.0%	100.0%
2000			
Professionals	14.5%	16.9%	19.8%
Managers	10.8	10.2	7.2
Sales Workers	7.0	7.0	6.5
Clerical Workers	18.4	14.9	11.4
Craftsmen	13.2	13.7	15.0
Operatives	15.6	15.6	16.5
Service Workers	12.6	13.4	14.7
Laborers	4.9	5.1	5.5
Farmers	3.0	3.2	3.4
Total	100.0%	100.0%	100.0%

[a,b]See Table 1.2.

direct labor coefficients were used in the IEA database, it is not sur-prising that the two sets of estimates for the economy as a whole are within 1% of each other.

The subsequent effects of automation are different for different types of work, and this is apparent even in terms of the nine broad cat-egories of labor shown in Tables 1.2 and 1.3.[4] By 1990 there is a pro-gressive increase in the proportion of professionals and a steep reduc-tion in the number and proportion of clerical workers as we move from Scenario S1 through S2 to S3.

By the year 2000, professionals will account for nearly 20% of all labor requirements under Scenario S3 compared to 15.6% in 1978, and demand for clerical workers falls to 11.5% from 17.8% in 1978. The demand for managers also slackens noticeably by 2000 under Scenario S3, and in absolute numbers is lower than that demand in 1990, even though in the aggregate 32 million workers have been added to the labor force by the end of the decade according to this scenario.

The increased demand for professionals is mainly for computer specialists (LAB #6–8)[5] and engineers (LAB #1–4) while the demand for all categories of clerical workers is significantly lower under Sce-nario S3 than S1.

The projected demand for construction craftsmen (LAB #25–28) has a markedly different pattern than that which has been discussed so far: it follows the cycles of the investment demand for structures, and the peaks under Scenario S3 reflect the increased demand for capital. The sharp fall in demand for skilled metal-workers (LAB #30–31) reflects in part the increased use of CNC machine tools.

The impact of robots on demand for the affected semi-skilled occu-pations (LAB #39–43, 46)[6] and Laborers (LAB #52) is much more modest. While the reduction in demand for these categories of workers which is directly attributable to robots is about 400,000 in 1990 and almost 2 million in 2000 under Scenario S3, the net demand is about the same as under Scenario S1, apparently due to the off-setting effects of increased production of capital goods. One effect of the automation

---

4. Most of the nine aggregate categories are self-explanatory. Craftsmen, operatives, and laborers are sometimes called skilled, semi-skilled, and unskilled blue-collar workers, respectively. The occupational classification scheme is given in Table B.9 of Appendix B.

5. LAB #mm refers to occupation number mm in the IEA occupational classification scheme (Table B.9 of Appendix B).

6. LAB #46, a residual category of operatives including semiskilled metal workers, is affected by both CNC machine tools and robots.

represented in Scenario S3 is reduced requirements for iron and fer-
roalloys (IEA #5 and 36),[7] due in part to reduced steel scrap attributable to the use of computer-numerically-controlled machine tools. At
the same time, the increased demand for nonferrous metals (IEA #6
and 37) is also notable.

For most sectors increases in output are accompanied by reductions in employment under Scenario S3 as compared to S1, particularly
for many of the metal-working sectors (e.g., IEA #37–44) and Semiconductors (IEA #58). While employment in the computer sector (IEA
#50) increases substantially, output grows at a much greater rate.
Under the given assumptions—in particular, the same final demand
(that does not include investment) for all three scenarios—the increase
in the actual output of most service sectors is about the same under
alternative scenarios, and the labor savings in the service sectors due to
office automation are very substantial, especially for IEA #71–75 and
83–85.

The proportion of employment absorbed in the production of capital goods varies considerably from occupation to occupation. While
there are differences over time and across scenarios, it appears that 5–
6% of the private economy labor force is employed directly or indi-
rectly in the production of the private economy's capital goods.[8] About
12–15% of craftsmen are involved in the production of capital goods,
9–11% of laborers, and a somewhat smaller percentage of operatives.
As could be anticipated, practically no agricultural workers and barely
1% of service workers are involved. While under most scenarios for
most years only 2–3% of professionals are so engaged, this rises to
slightly more than 4% by 2000 under Scenario S3.

Aggregate gross output is in all years several percent higher under
Scenario S3 (and S2) than S1. While most of the increase in output
under Scenario S3 relative to S1 is due to the production of intermediate goods (involving an indeterminate amount of "double-counting"),
by far the greatest percentage increase (in most years) is in the production of investment goods. In the year 2000, for example, aggregate
gross output is 6.6% higher under Scenario S3 than S1; final demand
(comprising personal consumption, government purchases, and net
exports but not productive investment) is postulated to be the same;

7. IEA #nn refers to sector number nn in the IEA sectoral classification scheme which is
given in Table B.1 of Appendix B.

8. These include capital for public education and health care but exclude other government capital. Also excluded from these figures are residential real estate and other household capital and business inventories which are all accounted for as part of final deliveries.

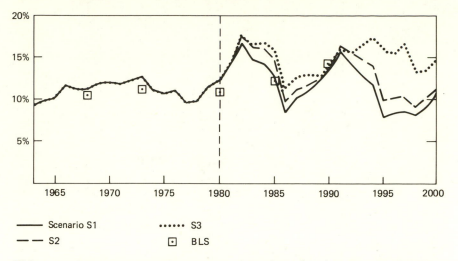

FIG. 1.1.   Investment as a Percentage of Total Final Deliveries, 1963–2000.

Note: Investment is defined as gross private fixed capital formation, including investment for public education and health care. Total final deliveries, as defined for this graph, include investment.

Source: BLS figures are given for 1968, 1973, 1980, 1985, and 1990 in U.S. Department of Labor (1982a, p. 14).

output for interindustry use is 8.8% higher, and investment is 42.3% higher. Figure 1.1 shows annual investment as a percentage of total final deliveries under the three scenarios over the period from 1963 to 2000; several BLS estimates and projections are also shown in the figure. The labor savings discussed earlier are in large part made possible by the substitution of capital for labor.

TABLE 1.4.   Total Investment and Investment in Computers and Robots Under Scenarios S1, S2, and S3 by Decade

	Gross investment by decade (millions of dollars, 1979 prices)			Computers as proportion of total
	Total	Computers	Robots	
1971–1980				
Scenarios S1, S2, and S3	$2,304,430	$34,584	$248	1.5%
1981–1990				
Scenario S1	3,552,491	68,204	1,870	1.9
Scenario S2	3,838,773	191,161	5.808	5.0
Scenario S3	4,069,842	330,228	10,687	8.1
1991–2000				
Scenario S1	4,103,334	86,480	2,338	2.1
Scenario S2	4,686,462	490,766	11,043	10.5
Scenario S3	6,151,903	1,191,765	29,078	19.4

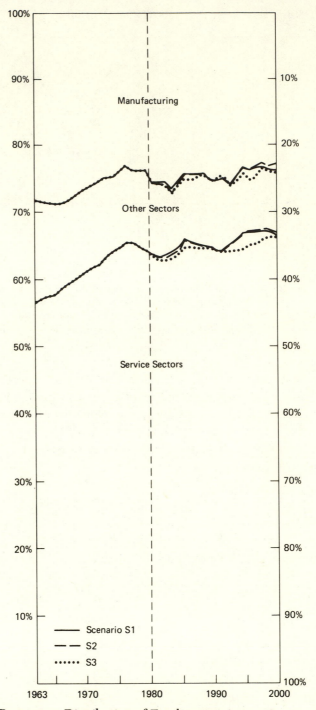

FIG. 1.2. Percentage Distribution of Employment Among Service, Manufacturing, and Other Sectors, 1963–2000

Note: Manufacturing is defined to include IEA #12–66 and #86. The residual category, Other Sectors, includes Agriculture (IEA #1–4), Mining (IEA #5–10), and Construction (IEA #11). All remaining sectors are classified as Services. Public administration, armed forces, and household workers are not included.

Capital flows under alternative scenarios are summarized in Table 1.4. Investment in this table is cumulated (in constant 1979 prices) over ten-year periods in an attempt to focus on secular changes rather than year-to-year fluctuations. The first three columns of the table show total investment, investment in computers, and investment in robots over three successive decades. During both decades 1981–1990 and 1991–2000, about half the value of the additional investment under Scenario S3 as compared with S1 (or S2) is for computers. Total investment is about 15% higher under Scenario S3 than S1 in the 1980s and 50% higher in the 1990s.

The increasing use of automatic equipment involves shifts not only in the occupational but also in the sectoral distribution of the work force, with the increased production of capital goods slowing the transfer from manufacturing to service sector employment over the next 20 years. This is seen in Figure 1.2, which is a graphic presentation of the percentage of employment in manufacturing, service, and other sectors between 1963 and 2000.

Discussion and Implications of the Results

Scenario S3, which is the basis for the following discussion, assumes the accelerated adoption through the year 2000 of computer-based automation into all sectors of the economy, accompanied by a continual increase in the material standard of living. While investment is computed within the IEA model, the other components of final demand (personal consumption, government purchases, and net exports) are prescribed as explained in Chapter 6. This section introduces an additional scenario, S4, with alternative final demand assumptions.

Table 1.5 shows final deliveries postulated under Scenario S3 on a per employee and per capita basis for selected years since 1963 and projections for 1990 and 2000. The range of figures shown for the future U.S. population corresponds to the most recent lowest and highest Bureau of the Census projections. Final demand per capita and its average annual rate of growth are likewise expressed as a range from highest (corresponding to the lowest population projection) to lowest (corresponding to the highest population projection). The last column of the table shows the real growth of per capita final demand which is postulated in Scenarios S1, S2, and S3 to increase over the next 20 years at about 2% a year under the high population projections.

The first row of Table 1.6 shows the levels of employment which

TABLE 1.5. Noninvestment Final Deliveries[a] per Employee-Year and per Capita Under Scenarios S3 and S4[b], 1963–2000.

	Final deliveries[a] (millions of dollars, 1979 prices)	Final deliveries[a] per employee-year (dollars, 1979 prices)	Population (millions)	Final deliveries[a] per capita (dollars, 1979 prices)	Average annual rate of growth in final deliveries[a] per capita since last benchmark year (%)
Scenario S3					
1963	$1,226,784	$19,189	189.2	$6,484	—
1967	1,442,482	20,725	198.7	7,260	2.87
1972	1,716,593	21,951	209.9	8,178	2.41
1977	1,883,452	21,850	220.2	8,553	0.90
1990	2,902,133	23,404	246–255	11,797–11,381	2.50–2.22
2000	3,855,045	24,680	256–282	15,059–13,670	2.47–1.85
Scenario S4[b]					
1990	2,782,565	24,133	246–255	11,311–10,912	2.2–1.9
2000	3,224,360	25,151	256–282	12,595–11,434	1.1–0.5

Sources: Final deliveries, see Chapter 6; population (U.S. Department of Commerce, 1979, 1982b, 1982c).

[a]Final deliveries include goods and services purchased from the private economy for personal and public consumption and net exports. They exclude gross private fixed nonresidential investment.

[b]See text for description of Scenario S4.

TABLE 1.6. U.S. Employment Under Scenarios S3 and S4,[a] 1963–2000, and Other Projections

	1963	1967	1972	1977	1990	2000
IEA employment[b] estimates and projections						
Scenario S3	62.8	69.6	78.2	86.2	124.1	156.6
Scenario S4	62.8	69.6	78.2	86.2	115.3	128.2
Actual and projected employment from other sources[b,c]	62.8	70.9	78.1	87.4	111.0–123.9	na
Actual and projected civilian labor force[d]	71.8	77.3	86.5	97.4	123.9–138.3	132.8–157.4

[a]See text for description of Scenario S4.

[b]Includes private sector employment (jobs) plus employment in public education and health. Excludes public administration, armed forces, and household workers.

[c]Entries for 1963–1977 are from U.S. Department of Commerce (1981, 1982a). The ratio of "business" employment (as defined in note 'a') to civilian labor force projected by the BLS for 1990 (U.S. Department of Labor, 1981) was applied to the civilian labor force projections for 1990 which are given in this table. The BLS has not projected figures for 2000. Figures for 1990 and 2000 are reported as a range from low to high.

[d]Entries for 1963–1977 are from U.S. Department of Labor (1980). The range of projections for 1990 and 2000 are based on the most recent population estimates summarized in U.S. Department of Commerce (1982b) and rates of participation in the labor force of the portion of the population over age 16 (U.S. Department of Labor, 1982a, Appendix C). The lowest projection, for example, is calculated from the lowest participation rate and the over-16 portion of the lowest population projection.

according to Scenario S3 would be required in order to satisfy this growth in total final deliveries (assumed in this as well as in Scenarios S1 and S2). The first four entries of the third row show data for the same employment concept prepared from government sources for benchmark years between 1963 and 1977, and the match with the IEA results is excellent. For 1990 the projection based on BLS assumptions (which are described in the notes to the table) is presented as a range of low to high. Since no comparable figures have been projected for 2000, we include in the last row of the table civilian labor force projections for the purpose of comparison with the IEA employment projections. The difference between the employment concept of the first three rows and the civilian labor force is that the latter measures persons rather than jobs and includes both the unemployed and those employed in households and public administration. For the years shown between 1963 and 1977, this difference amounts to between 6.5 and 10 million.[9]

Projected labor requirements under Scenario S3 for 1990 fall at the upper limit of the BLS-based projection of 124 million (and the latter assumes an exogenous unemployment rate of about 4%).

As we look further into the future, if the civilian labor force projections reported in the table are accepted,[10] the projected labor requirements of 156.6 million under Scenario S3 for the year 2000 exceed the available labor force (because even a maximum civilian labor force of 157.4 million must allow for public administration, household workers, and some multiple job-holders). Thus the rate of growth in final demand that has been assumed under Scenario S3, based on BLS projections, could not be achieved through only those aspects of technological change that have been represented in this scenario.

The fourth scenario, S4, was formulated to assess what future rates of growth of final demand could actually be attained within the constraints of available labor, according to current labor force projections, and under the technological assumptions of Scenario S3. For Scenario S4 we progressively reduced the level, while maintaining the compos-

9. Public administration is treated here as a final demand sector, and as such its future input structure is based on BLS projections. In future work, technological changes affecting public administration will be projected in terms of individual technological coefficients. Preliminary computations suggest that public administration employment would be about 15.6% less in 2000 under the technological assumptions of Scenario S3 than those of S1, compared to a difference of 11.7% between the two scenarios for employment in the private economy.

10. On the accuracy of such projections, see Keyfitz (1981) and Fullerton (1982).

iton, of final demand prescribed by Scenario S3 for 1990 and 2000 (and accordingly for years between 1980–1990 and between 1990–2000). For each sequence of final deliveries up to the year 2000, the corresponding labor requirements were computed. The procedure was repeated until the computed labor required for 1990 and for 2000 fell within the range of labor force projections reported in Table 1.6. Of course, with additional iterations one could ensure closing in on a prescribed level of final demand that would result in any specific labor force projection (e.g., the midpoints of the ranges shown in Table 1.6). Some results of Scenario S4 are presented in Tables 1.5 and 1.6.

When the value (in 1979 prices) of final demand—excluding investment—under Scenario S3 (based on BLS projections) is reduced by 4.4% in 1990 and 16.8% in 2000 (compare Scenarios S3 and S4, Table 1.5), the aggregate employment requirements under Scenario S4 fall within the range of the projected labor force (Table 1.6). Because overall economic activity is lower under Scenario S4 than S3, there will be less investment. For this reason the percentage reduction in the demand for labor as compared to that of Scenario S3 is even greater than that of final demand. For any given year, the occupational composition of employment turns out to be virtually identical under Scenarios S3 and S4, with a lower representation under S4 of those engaged particularly in the production of capital goods; for example, craftsmen represent 14.7% of the employed in 2000 compared to 15.0% under Scenario S3.[11]

Under Scenario S4, per capita final deliveries grow at about 2% a year through the 1980s and between 0.5–1.1% through the 1990s.[12] This is an estimate of the extent to which real per capita consumption will be able to increase over the next two decades if the entire projected labor force is employed using the progressively phased-in com-

11. In fact, all three scenarios (S1, S2, and S3) were recomputed with the new final demand projections (S4 is the one of the three corresponding to the technological assumptions of S3). All of the observations made earlier in this chapter comparing the results of Scenario S3 to S2 and S1 hold with the new, as well as the original, final demand projections, although the actual figures are of course different. After this study was completed, BLS released revised final demand projections (U.S. Department of Labor, 1984) which are even lower than those computed under Scenario S4. If Figure 1.1, showing investment as a proportion of total final demand, were redrawn for the three new scenarios, all three curves would be almost flat in the late 1990s. The lowering of final demand has this effect since new capital is introduced when capacity is expanded.

12. Fixed final deliveries are combined with high-growth and low-growth population projections. Thus the 1.1% rate of growth of per capita final deliveries corresponds to the low population projection, and 0.5% to the high population projection.

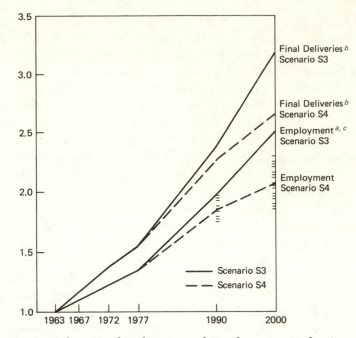

FIG. 1.3.   Growth in Final Deliveries and Employment[a] Under Scenarios S3 and S4, 1963–2000 (1963 = 1.0).
[a]See note *b*, Table 1.6
[b]See note *a*, Table 1.5
[c]Hashed lines (≡) show range of employment projections based on official sources. The range for 2000 assumes the same ratios of employment to civilian labor force as given in Table 1.6 for 1990.
Sources: Final Deliveries, Table 1.5. Employment, Table 1.6.

puter-based technologies. Figure 1.3 summarizes the differences in postulated aggregate final demand and resulting levels of employment between Scenarios S3 and S4.

Based on the findings presented in this report, it is not yet possible to pass a final verdict on the question of technological unemployment by the year 2000. Technological changes taken into account in the four scenarios described have been limited to computer-based automation. It will now be necessary to ascertain by means of equally detailed factual inquiry, and to incorporate into the technical matrices used in these projections, other types of change that are bound to take place, for example in agriculture and in the substitution of materials—like plastics for metals on the one hand and paper on the other. Moreover, we have explicitly excluded from our scenarios any major breakthroughs in computer technology that might affect significant numbers of workers before the year 2000. While it is likely to be at least 20 years before products embodying future breakthroughs in areas such as automatic programming, speech recognition, or three-dimensional robot vision are actually adopted on a large scale, some surprises are certainly possible.

The great industrial revolution inaugurated by the introduction of mechanical power continued to transform western economies and society over a period of some 200 years. The computer revolution became visible only a few years ago, and by the year 2000 it will be no more advanced than the mechanization of European economies had advanced by, let us say, the year 1820.

A major consideration in realizing the transition from the old to new technologies will be the availability of workers with the training and skills that match the work that needs to be done. According to Scenario S3, labor requirements to satisfy a continually but moderately increasing standard of living will number 124 million jobs in 1990 with the required occupational composition, reflecting the technologies that will be in place, given in Table 1.2. Let us suppose that there is an adequate total number of individuals to fill these jobs, but due to a very slow change in the orientation of education, training, guidance, and so on, these individuals' skills and occupational expectations will reflect the mix of jobs that corresponded to the technologies that were in place in 1978 (also shown in Table 1.2). Under these assumptions, 744,000 managers (0.6% of 124 million), and over 5 million clerical workers would be potentially unemployed in 1990 while there would be unfilled positions (in the same total amount under the present simple assumptions) in the other aggregate occupational categories. Of course some of those seeking managerial and clerical employment would be able to find jobs of other kinds but with obvious limitations on the degree of job mobility.

The same considerations apply within each broad occupational category. Among professionals, for example, the IEA employment projections for 1990 show a greater proportion of engineers and especially of computer specialists than in 1978. Among skilled workers, the projections include a higher proportion of foremen and production mechanics and a lower proportion of construction and metal-working craftsmen than in 1978.

The crude experiment described above provides of course only a very rough approximation of the ability of the future labor force to fulfill specific job requirements. An adequate evaluation will require comparably detailed analysis of the future structure of households and the job-related attributes of their members. This has not yet been carried out.

Concerted efforts in education and training can facilitate this shift in the occupational composition of the labor force. Scenario S3 requires that the production of electronic educational courseware grow in real terms at over 35% a year in the 1980s and over 10% in the 1990s. (The underlying assumptions about the use of computers in education are discussed at length in Chapter 4.) In the past, higher levels of "conventional" education in the U.S. relative to other countries also played a key role in the successful transformation of our labor force from mainly agricultural workers into a wide range of other occupations. As was the case in the past for conventional education, the growth and quality of computer-based education and its delivery will no doubt become an item of government policy and corporate and trade union strategies.

This study has taken a first systematic, albeit partial, glance at prospects for employment for 15 years into the future, a significant lengthening of the usual time horizon for economic inquiry. With the feasibility and fruitfulness the approach taken in this study now hopefully demonstrated, we need to extend and improve the sector studies on which the scenarios are based. Subsequently, it will be possible to investigate the impacts on the distribution of income implied by the technological assumptions (see Duchin, 1984). Eventually it will be necessary, instead of taking final deliveries as given, to formulate and implement a completely closed dynamic input-output model in which consumption and employment are determined simultaneously.

In the meantime, the framework developed for this study can profitably be used to investigate numerous critical economic issues which until now have not been subject to systematic inquiry.

Projections of Future Technologies

The overall implications for American workers of computer-based technologies depend upon the specific instances of technological change in each sector of the economy. Each of the remaining chapters in this book describes a different aspect of these changes both qualitatively and quantitatively.

The future production and use of computers is described in Chapter 2 as well as the future production and use of computer-numerically-controlled machine tools and robots, and the increasing integration of all three components on the factory floor. Computers will also be used increasingly to integrate the operations of various types of office equipment; the automation of paperwork is taken up in Chapter 3.

The computer can be expected to play a crucial role in the future of both formal and informal education. Specific scenarios about the educational use of computers in schools, on the job, and in households are described in Chapter 4. Chapter 5 addresses computer-related technological change in the large and growing health-care sectors. The final chapter describes the projections for all final deliveries (e.g., to government agencies) not explicitly taken up elsewhere.

Chapters 2 through 6 contain projections to 1990 and 2000 of the technical coefficients describing the future computer-based technological change, the consequences of which were analyzed in Chapter 1. These projections correspond to two detailed alternative scenarios which in general terms can be described as moderate (Scenario S2) and accelerated (Scenario S3) automation. All technical coefficients tabulated in these chapters are described in terms of their economic interpretations. These tables of numbers are intended to be a comprehensible statement of our technological assumptions. As such, they are also the parameters of the dynamic input-output model.

Each of the following chapters focuses on the production and use of a particular set of technologies which are introduced into the model of the economy after 1980 by changing the technical coefficients which described the economy in 1980. These technical coefficients are organized into four matrices:

A   intermediate input requirements per unit of output
B   capital requirements per unit increase in output
R   capital replacement requirements per unit of output
L   labor requirements per unit of output

The definitions of these matrices and their relationships within the dynamic input-output model are discussed in Appendix A. Data sources for these coefficients through 1980 are described in Appendix B.

The composition of a sector's capital stock in terms of individual tools and machines depends upon both the requirements of individual technologies and the pattern according to which new ones have in the past replaced old ones through modernization and expansion. While the technical requirements per unit increase in output of the newest technologies in a particular sector (our technical coefficients in the B matrices) can in many cases be projected in advance based on technical considerations, the future levels of economic activity are by contrast the outcome—not the input—of our analysis.

The interindustry and labor requirements per unit of sectoral output in turn depend upon the mix of capital equipment actually in place. The proper way to project these columns of coefficents for a particular sector is to construct them each year within the dynamic model as an appropriately weighted average of the columns corresponding to each technology in use, including the newest. While this idea is not new,[13] the associated conceptual and data problems have not yet been satisfactorily addressed. In this study we have made *a priori* projections of the intermediate and labor coefficients. The one exception is for the displacement of human labor by robots. Because there is virtually no existing stock of robots before 1980 (and because we make several other plausible simplifying assumptions), we are able to change the labor coefficients within the model on the basis of the numbers of robots actually accumulated between 1980 and 2000.

REFERENCES

Bezdek, Roger H., and Robert M. Wendling. 1976. Disaggregation of structural change in the American economy: 1947–1966. *The Review of Income and Wealth* 22 (June): 167–85.

Carter, Anne P. 1970. *Structural change in the American economy*. Cambridge, Mass.: Harvard University Press.

————. 1963. "Incremental Flow Coefficients for a Dynamic Input-Output Model with Changing Technology," in Tibor Barna (ed.), *Structural Interdependence and Economic Development*, New York: St. Martin's Press: 277–302.

Duchin, F. 1984. Automation and its effect on employment and income. In *American Jobs and the Changing Industrial Base*, ed. E. Collins and L. Tanner. Cambridge, Mass.: Ballinger Publishing Co.

Fullerton, Howard N. 1982. How accurate were projections of the 1980 labor force? *Monthly Labor Review* 105, no. 7 (July) 15–21.

Keyfitz, Nathan. 1981. The limits of population forecasting. *Population and Development Review* 7, no. 4 (December): 579–93.

Leontief, Wassily. 1941. *The structure of the American economy, 1919–1929*. Cambridge, Mass.: Harvard University Press.

Leontief, Wassily, Anne P. Carter, and Peter A. Petri. 1977 *The future of the world economy*. New York: Oxford University Press.

Osterreichisches Institut fur Wirtschaftsforschung and Osterreichische Akademie der Wissenschaften. 1981. *Mikroelektronik: Anwendungen, Verbreitung und Auswirkungen am Beispiel Osterreichs*. Wien: Springer-Verlag.

13. See, for example, A. P. Carter (1963).

U.S. Department of Commerce. Bureau of the Census. *Current Population Reports*. Series P–25, nos. 802, 920, 922. Washington, D.C. (May 1979, May 1982a, October 1982b).

U.S. Department of Commerce. Bureau of Economic Analysis. *The National Income and Product Accounts of the United States, 1929–1976 Statistical Tables*. Washington, D.C. (September 1981).

————. Revised estimates of national income and products accounts. *Survey of Current Business* 63 (July 1982c).

U.S. Department of Labor. Bureau of Labor Statistics. *Handbook of Labor Statistics*. Bulletin 2070. Washington, D.C. (December 1980).

————. *The National Industry Occupation Employment Matrix, 1970, 1978 and Projected 1990*. Bulletin 2086, 2 vols. Washington, D.C. (April 1981).

————. *Economic Projections to 1990*. Bulletin 2121. Washington, D.C. (March 1982a).

————. *BLS Economic Growth Model System for Projections to 1990*. Bulletin 2112. Washington, D.C. (April 1982b).

————. *Economic Projections to 1995*. Computer tape received March 1984. Contains projections for final demand input-output matrices, employment, and investment.

Vaccara, Beatrice N., and Nancy W. Simon. 1968. Factors affecting the postwar industrial composition of real product. In *The Industrial Composition of Income and Product*, ed. John Kendrick, 19–58. New York: National Bureau of Economic Research, distributed by Columbia University Press.

The Automation
of Manufacturing

General Motors, aware of the growing use of robots by Japanese auto makers, predicts that by 1987, 90 percent of all its new capital investments will be in computer-controlled machines.[1]

Digital computers have the capability of controlling and integrating increasingly complex sequences of manufacturing operations, providing a powerful replacement for the paper tape and punched card whose use for machine control dates to the beginning of the 19th century. This section provides a description of the underlying technologies, concentrating in particular on computer-numerically-controlled (CNC) machine tools and robotics. Likely progress through the year 2000 is explored, and later sections of this chapter contain a technical description of two alternative scenarios describing the future production and use of computers, CNC machine tools, and robots, respectively.

The discussion in this chapter concerns the use of computers in all sectors of the economy and the accompanying demand for directly related personnel. Implications for office-type operations—which are carried out in all sectors and which constitute the entire production process in some service sectors—are taken up in Chapter 3 which focuses on the work of clerical, sales, and managerial workers.[2]

The manufacturing processes examined in detail in this chapter are those mainly involving assembly, material handling, machine tending, and the different stages and forms of the processing of metals. This focus excludes the automation of agriculture and mining, many of the

1. Levitan and Johnson (1982, p. 12).

2. Many categories of professionals also use computers; we have assumed that over the period of this study, automation will improve the quality of their output but not affect the quantity of their jobs on a per unit of output basis except in the cases explicitly examined (i.e., in education and health care).

high throughput, continuous processing sectors like petroleum processing (which are already highly automated), and a handful of other
sectors with specific production characteristics (such as apparel).

Conventional manufacturing machines have long been programmed and controlled by devices such as limit switches and cams. In
the 1960s servo-controls based on feedback loops were introduced.
The numerically controlled (NC) tools of that decade had a specific
logic wired into them; in the 1970s it became possible for the logical
control to pass from the special purpose machine to a computer. With
this step came the prospect of carrying out, without human intervention, a series of operations involving various machines and work-
pieces—provided that all steps could be prespecified in unambiguous
detail.

Possibly the most significant innovation in machine tool design in
this century took place in the 1950s with the development of numerical
control for cutting and forming metals. NC eliminated the need for
templates, drill jigs, stops, and human operators (Duke and Brand,
1981, p. 31). It reduced machining time per part, the amount of scrap
produced, and set-up time and increased management control of the
work pace (Lund, 1978, p. 27; Frost and Sullivan, 1982, p. 196). However, despite expectations by many industry observers in the late 1950s
and early 1960s that these advantages would revolutionize the production process in metalworking industries, only 2% of the machine tools
in these industries had numerical controls by 1977.

The failure of the market for NC tools to materialize in the 1960s
can be attributed to the high initial investments (both in the tools and
in personnel) that were required, maintenance problems, programming
inflexibility, and manager and worker resistance to change (Lund,
1977, p. H-56). By the late 1970s these obstacles began to disappear.
Between 1963 and 1973 the NC share of the total number of machine
tools shipped had fluctuated between 0.6 and 1.0%. This figure rose to
1.6% in 1977, 2.1% in 1979, and 2.7% in 1980. Between 1972 and
1980, the NC share of the value of shipments of machine tools almost
doubled, from 13.4% to 26.6% (Lund, 1977, p. H-61; National
Machine Tool Builders Association, 1981, pp. 93, 100).

Increasing familiarity with programmable machines, improvements in their quality, and lower relative NC machine costs help
explain the expanded use of NC in the 1970s. At least as important,
however, was the introduction of control by digital computer
[computer-numerical-control (CNC)]. By 1981 almost all the NC tools
on the market were of the CNC variety. The replacement of taped

instructions with a visual display terminal providing programming capability increased the number of potential NC applications in large plants that had formerly used less flexible technologies (e.g., transfer lines) and in small plants for which the older NC equipment was too inflexible. Eventually CNC tools will be linked to a hierarchy of computers throughout the firm and with other programmable machines, notably robots, on the plant floor.

A robot is distinguished by its multijointed arm which permits it to displace a tool or workpiece to specified points or along a specified path and to carry out designated operations at those points. While the first industrial robot was available as early as 1959, the market expanded very slowly to perhaps a few hundred in use in the U.S. by 1970, and 4000 in 1980. Other countries entered this market both as producers and users later than the U.S., but some—notably Japan—have subsequently moved more quickly.

The current generation of robots is capable of loading and unloading CNC machine tools, die-casting machines, hammer-forging machines, etc.; spray painting on an assembly line; cutting cloth with a laser; making molds; manipulating tools such as welding guns and drills; and assembling simple mechanical and electrical parts (Ayres and Miller, 1983, p. 25[3]). To date, robots have been installed primarily to replace unattractive and often dangerous jobs in foundries and in welding and painting operations in auto and farm equipment assembly plants. More sophisticated machine loading and assembly robots are on the drawing board, and already assembly robots with some vision and tactile sensors are used in production, for example by IBM, General Dynamics Corporation, and Boeing (Marcus, 1983, p. D2). Increasingly, the stand-alone robot will be integrated with machine tools and other equipment into a computer-controlled system that is capable of combining product design (perhaps with input from a human at a video screen) with production planning and implementation (CAD/CAM—computer-aided design/manufacturing). Chips integrating sensors (and some actuators) onto the same silicon substrate as the electronic circuitry have been produced since the mid 1970s, especially for military applications. In the future it may be feasible to link these solid-state sensors with the controlling computer for industrial use (Allan, 1984).

The projections about the future automation of production contained in the following sections of this chapter assume an increased

---

3. Some of the historical information in this section is also drawn from Chapter 2 of this reference.

adoption of improved versions of technologies that are already known. We project the increased use of computers for a wide variety of purposes and the accelerated substitution of CNC for conventional machine tools, the increasing use of machining centers in which a single machine performs several operations, and computer-controlled integration of several CNC machines. We also anticipate the use of robots in an increasing number of sectors and for an increasing diversity of operations. However, as the reader will see by the magnitudes of the coefficient changes in the following sections, we do not consider that technical progress and economic incentives will lead to unmanned production by the year 2000.

Computers

The Production of Computers

Information processing in the office, machine control in the factory, and the integration of office and factory operations will become increasingly dependent over the next two decades upon a hierarchy of computers which range from the desktop variety, now costing less than $10,000, to large mainframe computers in the $12 million range. In the IEA industry classification, this equipment is produced by IEA #50 which corresponds to the Standard Industrial Classification (SIC) #3573. This sector is defined to exclude microprocessors which provide the memory and processing functions of a computer on a single semiconductor chip (produced by Semiconductors, IEA #58). Also excluded are special purpose microprocessor-based machines, such as word processors (produced by Office Equipment, IEA #51) and CNC controls for machine tools (produced by Electric Industrial Equipment and Apparatus, IEA #53).

The production of computers and semiconductors has undergone dramatic changes since the 1960s. As the composition of computer output has shifted from mainframes to smaller, standardized models, the industry has been able to substitute lower-cost mass production for batch techniques. The industry has also benefitted from increased productivity in the production of semiconductors accelerated in the 1970s by moving labor-intensive operations abroad and mechanizing the remaining stages of production (wafer fabrication). According to one report, the average selling price of an integrated circuit fell from $4.20

in 1967 to 63 cents in 1975 (1972 prices) (U.S. Department of Commerce, 1979, p. 50).

The intermediate input and labor requirements of the Computer (IEA #50) and Semiconductor (IEA #58) sectors used in this study reflect these structural changes. On the average, the 1972 intermediate input requirements per unit of output of the Computer sector were 48% of their 1967 value (in constant 1979 prices). By 1977 these requirements again fell by about 50%. The corresponding declines in labor requirements were 56 and 68%, respectively. The intermediate input and labor requirements for the production of Semiconductors fell by similar magnitudes. For all scenarios we assumed that intermediate and labor coefficients for sectors IEA #50 and IEA #58 would be further reduced by 30% in 1990 and another 30% in 2000. These estimates were extrapolated from the past trends.

The Use of Computers

Capital Coefficients

The historical database described in Appendix B furnished all the data through 1977 required for our analysis. However, new estimates were made for 1977 of the computer requirements per unit expansion of each sector's output.[4]

The national stock of computers for 1972 and for 1977 was estimated (at $10 billion and $17.5 billion in 1979 prices, respectively) from data provided by the U.S. Department of Commerce (1982, p. 173), and each sector's share was approximated by its share of specialized computer personnel who programmed and operated the mainframes that still dominated at that time. [Only 0.6% of the value of computers in use in 1977 were desktops (International Data Corporation, 1981).] These sectoral computer stocks were divided by corresponding sectoral outputs to provide a measure of the average use of computers per unit of output in 1972 and 1977. For 1972, we now had both the vector described above (computer requirements per average unit of output for each sector) and the computer row of the B matrix for 1972

---

4. The product composition of capital in the 1977 B matrix was based on the official 1972 Capital Flow Table, still the most recent one available. While this time lag affects all entries in the 1977 B matrix, it was felt that the computer row was probably the most urgently in need of revision and that it could be significantly improved even by the rough and ready procedures described below.

(computer requirements per unit increase in output, i.e., reflecting the newest technologies). For the actual 1972 outputs, the required computer stock was calculated to be 2.25 times higher according to the computer row of the 1972 B matrix. We interpreted this to mean that in 1972, state-of-the-art technologies required on the average 2.25 times more computer capability per unit of output than did the average of all technologies actually in use in the economy. Assuming that the same ratio held in 1977, we were able to produce the computer row (row 50) of the B matrix for 1977.

The corresponding coefficients for 1990 and 2000 were projected for each sector on the basis of its anticipated future information processing and machine control requirements. These coefficients were quantified in the following manner.

We estimated that for the economy as a whole, to produce a given set of outputs (the 1977 outputs) according to the most modern technologies computer requirements would grow at an average annual rate of 10% between 1977 and 1990 for Scenario S2 and 15% for Scenario S3 and at half these rates between 1990 and 2000. Ninety percent of this growth in computer requirements was assigned to general information processing and allocated among sectors according to their shares of white-collar workers in 1977. The remaining growth was assumed to be for machine control and was allocated among sectors according to their share of the stock of machine tools in 1977.

Using these procedures, the industries with the largest computer requirements per unit increase in output (i.e., computer capital coefficients) in 1977 were those producing electrical and electronic equipment (IEA #51–60), Instruments (IEA #64, 65), Ordnance and Aircraft (IEA #12, 62), financial services (Banking and Insurance, IEA #73, 74), and Education (IEA #83, 89). Industries with relatively low computer capital coefficients in 1977 included Agriculture (IEA #1, 2), Mining (IEA #7, 10), and several service industries (IEA #75, 79), as well as Construction (IEA #11), Food (IEA #13), and Lumber (IEA #19). The sectors with the largest increases in computer capital coefficients subsequent to 1977 are those with large information processing requirements whose operations tend to be conducted in small establishments: Retail Trade (IEA #72), Real Estate (IEA #75), Hotels (IEA #76), Amusements (IEA #80), and Education (IEA #83, 89). Most of the computer equipment that will be used by these industries will be desktop computers and electronic cash registers.

Table 2.1 shows 15 industries that were projected to have large computer capital coefficients in 1990 and 2000. Taking the Aircraft

TABLE 2.1. Capital Coefficients for Computers in the Sectors with the Largest Coefficients in 1990 and 2000 (Dollars per Dollar Increase in Capacity, 1979 Prices)

Code	Sector	1977	Scenario S2		Scenario S3	
			1990	2000	1990	2000
40	Screw Machine Products and Stampings	.006	.045	.079	.088	.192
46	Metalworking Machinery and Equipment	.011	.077	.136	.150	.326
47	Special Industry Machinery and Equipment	.009	.055	.096	.105	.227
49	Miscellaneous Machinery, except Electrical	.012	.103	.184	.203	.446
55	Electric Industrial Equipment and Apparatus	.005	.045	.080	.088	.193
57	Electron Tubes	.029	.076	.118	.128	.252
62	Aircraft and Parts	.045	.075	.103	.109	.191
64	Scientific and Controlling Instruments	.013	.050	.084	.092	.192
68	Communications, except Radio and TV	.018	.064	.105	.115	.239
72	Retail Trade	.006	.070	.127	.141	.311
73	Finance	.081	.162	.234	.250	.464
74	Insurance	.084	.141	.191	.203	.354
77	Business Services	.037	.088	.132	.143	.277
82	Health Services, excluding Hospitals	.008	.048	.084	.092	.198
84	Nonprofit Organizations	.010	.104	.189	.210	.463

industry (IEA #62) as an example, $45,000 in computers was required to increase capacity by $1 million in 1977; by 2000 this requirement will reach $191,000 under Scenario S3. The nine manufacturing industries shown in this table are among the earliest candidates for computer-based flexible manufacturing systems, e.g., Screw Machine Products (IEA #40), Metalworking Machinery (IEA #46), and Aircraft (IEA #62). The seven service sectors have significant information processing requirements and include Retail Trade (IEA #72), Finance (IEA #73), Insurance (IEA #74), and Business Services (IEA #77).

There are two different motivations for the purchase of capital goods to maintain existing capacity: replacement of nonoperational equipment that has either prematurely failed or exhausted its physical life, and the replacement of operational equipment by a more modern vintage. The total value of replacement capital per unit of a sector's output (i.e., a column total in the R matrix) was found to fluctuate relatively little over the period 1963 to 1977 and was in most cases projected to remain at its 1977 values through 2000. It was assumed that this would continue to cover the replacement of nonoperational equipment and some general modernization.

However, it is clear that computers and the other capital goods examined in this chapter will increasingly enter into use even in the absence of economic expansion. For this reason, the product composition of each column of the 1977 R matrix was altered in projecting it for 1990 and 2000. In particular, each sector's purchases of computers for replacement of existing capacity per unit of sectoral output were assumed to be as great as the average stock of computers per unit of output projected for each of those years.

LABOR COEFFICIENTS Many occupations have already been directly affected by the increasing use of computers in the production of goods and services. In this section we describe the method used to project future changes in the labor coefficients for three occupations (Programmers, LAB #6; Systems Analysts, LAB #7; and other Computer Specialists, LAB #8) which depend wholly upon the use of computers, and one occupation (Drafters, LAB #15) which is being eliminated by computers.

The labor coefficients for the three computer occupations in computer-using sectors[5] were calculated for 1990 and 2000 on the basis of projections of the number of computer workers required per unit of computer stock and of computer requirements per unit of output. Recent developments suggest that in the future the number of specialized computer personnel required for the effective use of a given amount of computational capability is likely to fall.

Table 2.2 shows aggregate ratios of computer workers to computer stock for the three computer occupations for the census years 1972 and 1977, and these ratios show substantial declines for all three computer occupations.

We assume that these ratios continue to fall until 1990. Such a trend is supported by a recent study by the International Data Corporation which found that among 350 computer users over the 1981–83 period, the share of the budget covering specialized staff has steadily

---

5. Projected coefficients for the computer occupations in the Computer sector (IEA #50) were described earlier.

TABLE 2.2. Aggregate Labor Requirements per Unit of
Computer Stock for Three Computer Occupations, 1972
and 1977 (Workers per Million Dollars, 1979 Prices)

Occupation	1972	1977
Programmers (LAB #6)	15.0	11.0
Systems Analysts (LAB #7)	11.6	9.0
Other Computer Personnel (LAB #8)	2.5	2.1

fallen while the computer room equipment portion has risen (Zientara, 1983, p.1). Under Scenario S2, advances in software and reductions in maintenance requirements were assumed to reduce specialized employment per computer to 67% of the 1977 ratio for each computer occupation in all sectors by 1990. Under Scenario S3, these advances were assumed to be more rapid, and the ratios were reduced to 33% of the 1977 figures. The ratios remain unchanged between 1990 and 2000 under both scenarios.

The labor coefficients for 1990 and 2000 were calculated by multiplying each ratio, sector by sector, by the corresponding average computer requirements discussed earlier. The industries with the largest 1990 and 2000 labor coefficients for Computer Programmers are listed in Table 2.3. The coefficients increase over time since increasing average computer requirements per unit of output more than offsets falling labor requirements per unit of computer stock.

In contrast to the future prospects of these three computer occupations, Drafters (LAB #15) are among those occupations which will be displaced by computers. In 1978 there were 296,000 Drafters, 90% of whom worked in private establishments preparing detailed drawings based on specifications provided by scientists, engineers, architects, and designers. Computer Aided Design (CAD) will eliminate all but the most skilled drafters and in addition increase the productivity of those who are not displaced. According to a Society of Manufacturing Engineers report (Kidd and Burnett, 1981, p. 1), "It has been proven conclusively many times that CAD can improve the productivity of the designer/draftsman by factors of between 2:1 and 5:1 depending upon the applications."

The labor coefficients for Drafters in 1990 and 2000 were projected by an equation that incorporates these two effects:

$$1_{qj}^{t} = \alpha(1 - \beta)(1 - \gamma)\, 1_{qj}^{77} + (1 - \alpha)\, 1_{qj}^{77} \qquad (2\text{-}1)$$

TABLE 2.3. Labor Coefficients for Computer Programmers in the Sectors with the Largest Coefficients in 1990 and 2000 (Workers per Million Dollars of Output, 1979 Prices)

Code	Sector	1977	Scenario S2		Scenario S3	
			1990	2000	1990	2000
46	Metalworking Machinery and Equipment	.060	.241	.417	.230	.492
49	Miscellaneous Machinery, except Electrical	.055	.290	.523	.290	.639
51	Office Equipment, except IEA #50	.235	.296	.415	.222	.400
57	Electron Tubes	.166	.247	.351	.188	.344
72	Retail Trade	.027	.190	.342	.189	.417
73	Finance	.151	.333	.536	.293	.597
74	Insurance	.174	.286	.436	.236	.462
77	Business Services	.435	.905	1.470	.804	1.650
81	Hospitals	.044	.199	.337	.185	.393
83	Educational Services	.243	1.430	2.280	1.240	2.510
84	Nonprofit Organizations	.061	.283	.503	.278	.609
85	Government Enterprises	.021	.239	.436	.242	.538
89	Public Education	.243	1.430	2.280	1.240	2.510

where 1^t_{qj} is the labor requirement for Drafters per unit of output of sector j at time t; 1^{77}_{qj} is the labor coefficient for the base year (1977); α is the share of Drafters affected by CAD; β is the share of affected Drafters who are replaced by CAD; and γ measures the increase in drafter productivity attributable to CAD. Requirements for drafters unaffected by CAD (second term of the right-hand side of the equation) are added in to produce the new coefficients.

We assumed under Scenario S2 that 50% of all Drafters will be affected by CAD by 1990, while 90% are affected under Scenario S3. In the year 2000, the share of Drafters affected rises to 90 and 100%, respectively. By 1990, 20% of the affected Drafters are assumed to be replaced under Scenario S2 and 80% under S3. In 2000, these figures are 50 and 100%, respectively. Finally, we assumed that CAD improves the productivity of Drafters who use it by a factor of three. Since one Drafter using CAD can perform the work of three Drafters using conventional methods, labor requirements decline to 33% of their previous level, a reduction (γ) of 67%. These assumptions are summarized in Table 2.4.

TABLE 2.4.   Impact of Computer-Aided Design on Labor Coefficients for Drafters in 1990 and 2000[a]

	Scenario S2		Scenario S3	
	1990	2000	1990	2000
Proportion of Drafters (LAB #15) affected by CAD (α)	.50	.90	.90	1.00
Proportion of affected Drafters replaced by CAD (β)	.20	.50	.80	1.00
Reduction in Drafter requirements attributable to CAD (γ)	.67	.67	.67	.67
Labor coefficients for Drafters as proportion of 1977 coefficient	.63	.25	.16	.00

[a]Parameters in this table are used in equation (2-1).

As the last row of the table indicates, under Scenario S2 the labor coefficient for Drafters declines to 63% of the base year coefficient in 1990 and falls to 25% of the base year coefficient in 2000. With a larger share of Drafters affected and displaced under Scenario S3, the coefficient is only 16% of the base year coefficient in 1990. Under this scenario, no human drafters are required by the year 2000.

Computer-Numerically-Controlled (CNC) Metalworking Equipment

The Production of CNC Metalworking Equipment

One of the major impacts on future input requirements of the Metalworking Machinery sector (IEA #46) will be the increasing shift in product mix toward CNC tools. For present purposes we assume that the only difference in inputs between the conventional and CNC tool is in the control system.

In the early stages of CNC development, the controller was a minicomputer whose cost, according to an unpublished BLS case study, was somewhat less than 20% of the total CNC machine tool price. As microprocessors replaced the minicomputer, the cost of the controller dropped to about 10% of the total price (Frost and Sullivan, 1981, p. 4). The principal manufacturers of CNC controls are electronics and machine tool firms such as General Electric, Allen-Bradley, and Cincin-nati Milacron; and the individual establishments in which they are pro-duced are classified in the input-output tables as Industrial Controls, a component of the broader sector, Electric Industrial Equipment and Apparatus (IEA #53).

The requirements for industrial controls (from IEA #53) per unit of output of Metalworking Machinery (IEA #46) for 1990 and 2000 was calculated as

$$a^t_{53,46} = \alpha\beta^t + (1 - \gamma)a^{77}_{53,46} \qquad (2\text{-}2)$$

where α is the portion of the price of a CNC machine tool correspond-ing to its control unit; β is the portion in value of the output of IEA #46 which corresponds to CNC machine tools; and γ is the portion of the purchases from IEA #53 in the base year that correspond to inputs other than CNC control units. We estimated α at 10% for 1990 and 2000, and γ was assigned its 1977 value of 0.988. Estimation of β is described below.

The share of CNC machine tools by value in the output of IEA #46, β, grew at about 9% a year from 13.4% in 1972 to 20.2% in 1977 and 26.6% in 1980. Under Scenario S2 we assumed it would continue to increase by 9% a year through 1990 to 63% and then by 3% a year arriving at 85% in 2000. Under Scenario S3 we assumed that the share of CNC Machine tools in the output of IEA #46 would increase at 12% a year through 1990 to 83%, and that by 2000 it would arrive at 95% of the market.[6]

Under these assumptions, the coefficient $a_{53,46}$ increases from 0.019 in 1977 to 0.092 by 2000 under Scenario S2 and to 0.102 under Sce-nario S3. The coefficient and its components are shown in Table 2.5.

The Use of Metalworking Machinery

Capital Coefficients

Metalworking Machinery (IEA #46) includes nine 4-digit SIC indus-tries that produce both machine tools and the tools and dies and other accessories and equipment that are used in conjunction with them. The procedures used to produce the capital coefficients governing the

---

6. These four figures are shown in Table 2.6 which in its first four rows and footnotes summarizes all the assumptions that have been made about CNC machine tools.

TABLE 2.5.   Purchases of Electrical Industrial Equipment (IEA #53) per Unit of Output by Metalworking Machinery (IEA #46) in 1990 and 2000[a] (Dollars per Dollar, 1979 Prices)

	Scenario S2		Scenario S3	
	1990	2000	1990	2000
CNC controls per unit of output of Metalworking Machinery (IEA #46) $\alpha\beta^t$	.063	.085	.083	.095
Electrical Equipment (IEA #53) requirements per unit of output Metalworking Machinery (IEA # 46), except Industrial Controls $(1 - \gamma)\, a_{53,46}^{77}$	.007	.007	.007	.007
Electric Industrial Equipment (IEA # 53) requirements per unit output of Metalworking Machinery (IEA #46) in year t $(a_{53,46}^t)$	.070	.092	.090	.102

[a]Parameters in this table are used in equation (2-2).

investment demand for Metalworking Machinery are similar to those already described for computers.

To produce these coefficients and for use in subsequent computations, we need to compare CNC and conventional machine tools in terms of both value and productive capability. We estimated that the price of the average CNC tool in 1979 was 11 times that of the average conventional tool (National Machine Tool Builders Association, 1981, pp. 93, 100, 106). We also assumed that the average CNC tool can produce the same flow of output as 4.5 conventional tools, an estimate that lies within the range found in the literature. According to one source, "a CNC flame cutter does the work of 3–5 conventionally operated flame cutters" (*Iron Age*, 1980, p. 16). Another publication cites a U.S. firm that replaced 12 conventional lathes with 3 NC lathes (Real, 1980, p. 53), and an MIT study reports ratios of 3:1 and 5:1 (Lund, 1978, p. 25). The increasing use of machining centers (multipurpose milling machines) will tend to increase these ratios; according to Frost and Sullivan (1982), sales of NC machining centers will outpace other NC tools and will account for 33% of the total machine tool market by 1990. Therefore, we chose a figure (4.5) at the high end of the range.

The gross value of all metalworking machinery[7] in the U.S. in 1972 and 1977, given by the U.S. Department of Commerce (1982, p. 170), was transformed from purchasers' to producers' prices based on data about 1972 trade and transportation margins (U.S. Department of Commerce, 1980, p. A.23) and inflated to 1979 prices. This resulted in a stock valued at $125 billion in 1977. For each of the two years, the stock was distributed among sectors based on information about the number of conventional and NC tools held by each sector (Allan, 1978, pp. 136–7; National Machine Tool Builders Association, 1981, p. 256) and the estimate that the 1979 price of the average NC tool was 11 times that of the average conventional tool.

About 85% of the machine tools in use in the U.S. in 1978 were held by metalworking sectors (National Machine Tool Builders Association, 1981, p. 256). In the IEA classification, these 33 sectors are IEA #12, 22, 35–49, 51–57, 59–66, and 86. The assumptions described below about the accelerated adoption of CNC apply to these sectors. The remaining 15% of Metalworking Machinery was allocated to those nonmetalworking industries with the largest investment in machine tools in 1972 (the most recent date for which this information was available): Livestock (IEA #1), Other Agricultural Products (IEA #2), Construction (IEA #11), Lumber and Wood Products (IEA #19), Rubber (IEA #31), Glass (IEA #34), and Stone and Clay Products (IEA #35). The distribution of the stock among these sectors was based on the proportion of NC and conventional units using information from the 1976–78 American Machinist Inventory of Metalworking Equipment (*American Machinist*, 1978, pp. 136–7).

Average stock to output requirements were computed for 1972 and 1977 by dividing the value of each sector's stock by the corresponding output. Row 46 of the *B* matrix for 1972 represented metalworking equipment requirements per unit increase in each sector's output, with the element by element ratio (of row 46 of the *B* matrix to the average stock to output requirements) corresponding to the difference between most modern and average technologies. The same ratios were applied to the average requirements of 1977 to arrive at row 46 of the 1977 *B* matrix.

To project the capital coefficients for metalworking equipment in the metalworking sectors to 1990 and 2000, we assumed that a portion

---

7. Gross rather than net stocks were used for present purposes, where the interest is in capacity to produce, since the physical deterioration of metalworking machinery is considerably more gradual than its economic depreciation.

(α) of new output would be produced by CNC tools only and that the remainder $(1 - \alpha)$ would continue to use the 1977 mix of conventional and CNC (including NC) tools. The new coefficient was computed as

$$b_{46j}^t = \alpha^t b_{46j}^n + (1 - \alpha^t) b_{46j}^{77} \qquad (2\text{-}3)$$

where b_{46j}^n is the coefficient for CNC tools only.

In the metalworking sectors, CNC (including a small amount of NC) machine tools already accounted in value for 10.2% of the total machine tool stock in 1972 and 22.2% in 1977. We projected this percentage to grow by 5% a year to 42% in 1990 and to 85% in 2000 under Scenario S2. Under Scenario S3, the corresponding projections are 77% in 1990 and 95% in 2000. These proportions of CNC tools are assumed to be attained by each sector using metalworking equipment.

Since the CNC machine tool, estimated at 11 times the price of a conventional tool in 1979 prices, can be expected to replace 4.5 conventional tools, each using sector will require 2.44 ($11 \div 4.5$) times as much metalworking capital (in value) if it uses exclusively CNC *versus* exclusively conventional metalworking equipment. Thus the capital coefficient corresponding to the exclusive use of CNC tools (b_{46j}^n) was calculated as 2.44 times the coefficient corresponding to the exclusive use of conventional tools. (The latter coefficient is the 1972 coefficient adjusted to transform the small amounts of CNC tools then in use in each sector to the equivalent value of conventional tools.)

The projected Metalworking Machinery capital coefficients for 1990 and 2000 can be computed based on the information described above. These sector-specific coefficients can be summarized by reporting the aggregate capital requirements, according to these coefficients, to produce the 1977 outputs.

The assumptions discussed above are summarized in rows (1) to (3) of Table 2.6. While the exact proportion is different for each sector, the last row of Table 2.6 shows the average rate (weighted by the composition of 1977 outputs) by which the projected coefficients exceed the 1977 Metalworking Machinery capital coefficients.

Intermediate Input Coefficients

While the primary advantages of CNC tools lie in higher rates of machine throughput (output per hour of operation), reduced labor requirements, and their ability to be linked with other programmable machines thereby increasing the productivity of the entire process, the savings in materials through lower scrap rates is also often cited as a

TABLE 2.6. Impact of CNC Controls on Capital Requirements for Metalworking Machinery (IEA #46) in 1990 and 2000[a]

	Scenario S2		Scenario S3	
	1990	2000	1990	2000
Proportion of CNC tools in aggregate stock of Metalworking Machinery				
(1) in value	.42	.85	.77	.95
(2) in number of tools	.06	.34	.23	.65
(3) Proportion of all sectoral outputs produced using CNC tools (α^t)	.22	.70	.57	.89
(4) CNC tools as proportion in value of output of Metalworking Machinery	.63	.85	.83	.95
(5) Capital requirements for Metalworking Machinery to produce 1977 outputs using new coefficients (b^t_{46j}) as proportion of requirements based on 1977 coefficients (b^{77}_{46j})	1.33	2.01	1.83	2.28

[a]The first row of numbers (1) is projected. Then the second and third rows [(2) and (3)] are calculated based on the presumed relative prices of CNC to conventional tools of 11:1 and the presumed output to tool ratio of 4.5:1. On the average (i.e., weighted by the relative sectoral importance in the 1977 vector of outputs) the projected capital coefficients are larger than those of 1977 by the ratios given in the last row (5) of the table. The projections shown in the fourth row (4) were used earlier in determining the input structure of IEA #46 and are included here so all the assumptions can be examined simultaneously. The parameter α^t is used in equation (2-3).

key factor justifying the purchase of these tools. (See Lund, 1977, p. 27; Real, 1980, p. 138.)

As CNC tools are substituted for conventional tools, the use of Steel (IEA #36) per unit of output of the metalworking industries can be expected to decline. The new steel coefficients (a^t_{36j}) were computed as

$$a^t_{36j} = (1 - \alpha^t\beta\gamma)a^{77}_{36j} \tag{2-4}$$

where a^{77}_{36j} is the coefficient governing the use of steel per unit of output of sector j in 1977; α^t is the average proportion of output produced, and therefore of steel processed, by CNC tools; β is the reduction in steel scrap attributable to processing by CNC versus conventional tools; and γ is scrap as a proportion of purchased steel in 1977.

We assumed that the use of CNC tools can reduce steel waste from machining as well as the steel embodied in defective products by 70%

($\beta = 0.7$). We estimated that the production of scrap amounts to 25% of the value of the steel purchased for use with conventional equipment ($\gamma = 0.25$), which is somewhat higher than the Office of Technology Assessment (U.S. Congress, 1979, p. 27) estimate of 17.6% for the losses from machining plus the scrap that is purchased from end-product manufacture. The parameter α^t was projected based on data discussed in the last section.

These parameters are shown in Table 2.7. As a result of the reduction in steel scrap, we estimate that the coefficients will decline to 88% of their 1977 values by 2000 under Scenario S2, and to 84% under Scenario S3.

Labor Coefficients

The occupations most affected by the substitution of CNC for conventional tools are Machinists (LAB #30), Tool and Die Makers (LAB #31), and metalworking operatives [included in Other Operatives, (LAB #46)]. The labor coefficients for these three metalworking occupations in the 33 metalworking sectors were projected using the formula

$$e_q^t = (1 - \alpha^t\beta^t)e_q^{77} \qquad (2\text{-}5)$$

where α^t is the CNC share of the machine tool stocks (in units) in year t, β^t is the proportion of labor saved per unit of output through the use of CNC tools, q refers to one of the occupations, and e_q^{77} is the labor required per unit of output in 1977.

The share of CNC tools in the stock of machine tool units (α^t) increased at an average annual rate of 19% between 1977 and 1980. Projected future values were given in Table 2.6: under Scenario S2 this share increases at an annual rate of 8% between 1980 and 1990, from 2.7 to 6.0%. Under Scenario S3, the rate of increase is 24%, bringing the CNC share to 23%. In the year 2000 CNC tools are assumed to be 34% of the total stock under S2 and 65% under S3.

The labor savings per unit of output obtained with the use of CNC relative to conventional tools (β^t) results from the reduced labor requirements per tool and the increased output per tool (each CNC tool is assumed to be 4.5 times as productive as a conventional tool). The use of CNC tools will reduce the time required of operators on each machine for various reasons. According to Duke and Brand (1981, p. 31):

TABLE 2.7.   Impact of CNC Tools on Steel Requirements in 1990 and 2000[a]

	Scenario S2		Scenario S3	
	1990	2000	1990	2000
Reduction in steel scrap attributable to CNC tools (β)	.70	.70	.70	.70
CNC share of metalworking operations (α^t)	.22	.70	.58	.90
Scrap produced with conventional tools (γ) as proportion of a_{36j}^{77}	.25	.25	.25	.25
Steel coefficient (a_{36j}) as a proportion of coefficient in 1977	.96	.88	.90	.84

[a]Parameters in this table are used in equation (2-4).

In machining centers, complex shapes may be made by mounting cutting tools of varying sizes and power configurations on a single spindle. The cutting tools then are automatically changed by transfer arms, which also store the tool. The automatic tool changes take only a few seconds; formerly several minutes of an operator's time were required. Machining centers also eliminate the need to design, build and store the jigs and fixtures needed by single-purpose machines.

Single-purpose machines also have been much improved by numerical controls. For example, numerically controlled boring machines have reduced downtime for loading and unloading by up to 30%. Numerical control applied to grinding machines often halves layout time; programmable electronic wheel feed and wheel retraction have been developed which reduce labor time and enhance precision. The design of hobs for gear cutting has been subjected to computer calculation, saving cutting time.

Under Scenario S2, we assume that average CNC labor requirements per tool are 80% of the conventional tool requirements in 1990 and 60% in 2000; under Scenario S3 we assume values of 70% in 1990 and 50% in 2000. The ratio of the labor saving to the increased output per tool gives the relative labor requirements per unit of output using CNC versus conventional tools.

The values of the parameters and the resulting coefficients are presented in Table 2.8. The coefficients for all three occupations (LAB #30, 31, 46) were projected with the same method; the slightly higher proportions shown in the fourth row of the table reflect the fact that only 75% of the Other Operatives (LAB #46) category are affected (i.e., machine operators).

TABLE 2.8.   Impact of the Use of CNC Tools on Labor Coefficients (LAB #30, 31, and part of 46) in 1990 and 2000[a]

	Scenario S2		Scenario S3	
	1990	2000	1990	2000
CNC share in number of units of machine tool stock (α^t)	.06	.34	.23	.65
Labor requirements per CNC tool relative to conventional tool (ϕ^t)	.80	.60	.70	.50
Output per CNC tool relative to conventional tool (γ)	4.50	4.50	4.50	4.50
Proportion of labor saved per CNC tool $(\beta^t = 1 - \phi^t/\gamma)$	.82	.87	.84	.89
Labor coefficients for Machinists (LAB #30) and Tool and Die Makers (#31) as proportion of 1977 coefficient $(1 - \alpha^t\beta^t)$	.95	.70	.80	.42
Projected labor coefficients for Other Operatives (LAB #46) as a proportion of 1977 coefficient	.96	.77	.85	.56

[a]Parameters in this table are used in equation (2-5).

Robots

Because of the very small number of industrial robots in use until the last few years, Robotics (IEA #86) is not yet a separate sector in the SIC or other government classification schemes. Most of the data described in this section, especially on the use of robots, refers to the period 1980–82. We assume that the sector first began producing output on a commercial scale in 1977. While the extent and pattern of use of robots changes significantly under Scenarios S2 and S3, we assume no changes in the input structure for their production.

According to a report of the Japan Industrial Robot Association (JIRA), manufacturing industries are expected to account for 87% of the demand for industrial robots in Japan as late as 1990 (*Japan Economic Journal*, 1981, p. 7). Since Japan is pioneering the application of industrial robots to nonmanufacturing tasks, it is likely that an even higher share of robots will be confined to the manufacturing sector in the United States. In this report we do not consider their future use in agriculture, mining, and service sectors, or in the home.

We estimate the cost of an average robot at $70,000 in 1979

prices.[8] We further assume that the average industrial robot includes specific peripheral equipment that is passed along by Robotics (IEA #86), increasing the unit price by 20% to $84,000.

The Production of Robots

Capital Coefficients

Although robots have much in common with machine tools, metal fabrication plays a key role in the production process of Metalworking Machinery (IEA #46) while robots are manufactured primarily by assembling purchased components. The process used to manufacture computers, like that of robotics, is dominated by the assembly of relatively small parts (including electronic components). We used the 1972 capital coefficients of the Computer sector (IEA #50) for the Robotics sector with a single exception: the computer requirements of the Computer sector ($b_{50,50}$) were judged to be too large, and this coefficient was replaced by the coefficient that describes the purchases of computers by the Metalworking Machinery sector ($b_{50,46}$). The resulting column of capital requirements per unit increase in output of the Robotics sector (column 86 of the B matrix) is shown in Table 2.9.

Intermediate Input Coefficients

Our estimates of the intermediate input requirements for the production of robots were based on data for a comparable sector from the A matrix for 1977. Despite the differences in their capital requirements, the mix of requirements for materials and parts is similar to that of Metalworking Machinery and Equipment (IEA #46) with major exceptions concerning purchases of industrial controls (from IEA #53), Steel (IEA #36), and peripheral equipment (from IEA #45).

The controller is a key component of all robots, and various sources suggest 7% as the share of controls in the value of a robot. These controls are purchased from Electrical Industrial Equipment (IEA #53). We have assumed that the computer interface or microprocessor component of a robot is included in the controller and consequently no

8. This is consistent with estimates in the trade literature. Dividing Aron's estimate of the value of the 1980 robot market by the number of robots implies a unit price of $78,000 (Aron, 1982, p. 32). A similar calculation using Conigliaro's estimates implies a 1980 price of $68,966 (1981, p. 8).

TABLE 2.9.   Largest Capital Requirements for the Expanded Production of Robotics (Capital per Unit Increase in Capacity, 1979 Prices)

Code	Sector	Capital coefficient
22	Other Furniture and Fixtures	.0253
45	Materials Handling Machinery and Equipment	.0974
46	Metalworking Machinery and Equipment	.0491
47	Special Industry Machinery and Equipment	.0522
48	General Industrial Machinery and Equipment	.0386
50	Electronic Computing and Related Equipment	.0114
51	Office Equipment, except IEA #50	.0080
52	Service Industry Machines	.0071
53	Electric Industrial Equipment and Apparatus	.1424
56	Radio, TV, and Communications Equipment	.0682
60	Miscellaneous Electrical Machinery and Supplies	.0078
61	Motor Vehicles and Equipment	.0617
65	Optical, Ophthalmical, and Photographic Equipment	.0208
71	Wholesale Trade	.0415
72	Retail Trade	.0093

direct purchases are made by Robotics from the Computer and Semi-conductor sectors.

The use of steel per unit of output in the machine tool industry (0.077) was significantly reduced to reflect the primary role of assembly of purchased parts in the robot manufacturing process. Purchases from Primary Iron and Steel Manufacturing (IEA #36) are assumed to be 2 cents per dollar of robots (0.02) in 1979 prices. This compares to a figure of 1.2 cents (0.012) that can be derived from other estimates (Hunt and Hunt, 1982, Table 2.3).

A large part of the costs of a fully installed robot consists of materials-handling equipment and end-of-arm tooling. We assumed that the robotics industry purchases this equipment and passes it along to the buyer with the robot. Based on a study by Tanner and Adolfson (Hunt and Hunt, 1982, pp. 36–7), we estimate that 15% of the value of the robot (including the passed along robot-related equipment) consists of materials-handling equipment (primarily conveyors, part orienters, and guard rails) manufactured by Materials Handling Machinery and Equipment (IEA #45). In addition, 5% of the value of a robot is estimated to consist of end-of-arm tooling, purchased from the machine tool accessories portion of Metalworking Machinery (IEA #46). We assumed that

TABLE 2.10. Intermediate Requirements for the Robotics Sector in 1977 (Dollars per Dollar, 1979 Prices)

Code	Sector	Coefficients[a]
30	Petroleum Refining and Allied Industries	.0175
31	Rubber and Miscellaneous Plastic Products	.0042
35	Stone and Clay Products	.0042
36	Primary Iron and Steel Manufacturing	.0200[b]
37	Primary Nonferrous Metals Manufacturing	.0150
39	Heating, Plumbing, and Structural Metal Products	.0050
40	Screw Machine Products and Stampings	.0050
41	Other Fabricated Metal Products	.0066
45	Materials Handling Machinery and Equipment	.1500[c]
46	Metalworking Machinery and Equipment	.0558[d]
48	General Industrial Machinery and Equipment	.0133
49	Miscellaneous Machinery, except Electrical	.0220
53	Electric Industrial Equipment and Apparatus	.0800[e]
55	Electric Lighting and Wiring Equipment	.0008
60	Miscellaneous Electrical Machinery and Supplies	.0008
61	Motor Vehicles and Equipment	.0017
64	Scientific and Controlling Instruments	.0025
67	Transportation and Warehousing	.0092
68	Communications, except Radio and TV	.0042
70	Electric, Gas, Water, and Sanitary Services	.0083
71	Wholesale Trade	.0208
73	Finance	.0050
74	Insurance	.0017
75	Real estate and rental	.0075
76	Hotels, Personal, and Repair Services exc. Auto	.0017
77	Business Services	.0208
78	Eating and Drinking Places	.0083
79	Automobile Repair Services	.0008

[a]The source of these coefficients is the 1977 IEA column for Metalworking Machinery (IEA #46) in 1979 prices unless otherwise noted. See text for further explanation.

[b]Reduced from 0.077.

[c]This represents the Materials Handling Equipment that is passed along to the purchaser.

[d]Includes 0.05 for end-of-arm tooling and 0.0058 for other inputs from Metalworking Machinery (IEA #46).

[e]Includes 0.07 for controls and 0.01 for other purchases from IEA #53.

the value of this type of equipment accompanying the robot, that would otherwise have been purchased directly by robot-using sectors, is negligible in size and made no compensating adjustments. With these changes, the inputs increase by 20% of the value of Robotics output. To compensate for this increase, the remaining coefficients were divided by 1.20.

TABLE 2.11. Labor Coefficients for the Robotics Sector in 1982 (Workers per Million Dollars of Output, 1982 Prices)

Code	Occupation	Occupational composition	Corresponding labor coefficients
1	Electrical Engineers	12.1%	1.10
2	Industrial Engineers	2.2	.20
3	Mechanical Engineers	4.4	.40
4	Other Engineers	8.3	.75
6	Computer Programmers	2.1	.19
7	Computer Systems Analysts	.9	.08
8	Other Computer Specialists	.3	.03
9	Personnel & Labor Relations Workers	.3	.03
16	Other Professional, Technical	8.2	.74
17	Managers, Officials, Proprietors	9.0	.82
18	Sales Workers	4.0	.36
19	Stenographers, Typists, Secretaries	5.6	.51
20	Office Machine Operators	.9	.08
24	Other Clerical	9.2	.83
26	Electricians	.9	.08
29	Foreman, nec	.8	.07
30	Machinists	2.3	.21
32	Other Metalworking Craft Workers	1.5	.14
33	Mechanics, Repairers	.8	.07
39	Assemblers	14.7	1.34
40	Checkers, Examiners, Inspectors	2.8	.25
41	Packers and Wrappers	.4	.04
42	Painters	.7	.06
43	Welders, Flame Cutters	.9	.08
46	Other Operatives	5.6	.51
48	Janitors and Sextons	.4	.04
52	Laborers	.7	.06
	Total	100.0%	9.07

Table 2.10 shows the resulting intermediate input coefficients for Robotics. Major purchases are from four sectors: Electrical Industrial Equipment (IEA #53, for industrial controls and electric motors); Miscellaneous Machinery (IEA #49, for hydraulic and pneumatic cylinders and other parts); General Industrial Machinery (IEA #48, for hydraulic and pneumatic motors and power transmission equipment); and Primary Iron and Steel (IEA #36). The other large inputs, Material Han-

dling Machinery (IEA #45) and Metalworking Machinery (IEA #46) consist of robot-related equipment that is passed along to the using industry.

Labor Coefficients

Estimates of the labor required per unit of output in the Robotics industry were based on discussions with the personnel department of Unimation, Inc., the firm that at present accounts for almost half the robots produced in the U.S. Table 2.11 shows that four occupations account for most of the employment: Engineers (27%), Managers (9%), Clerical Workers (16%), and Assemblers (15%). The occupational composition reported by Unimation for 1982 was assumed for the robotics industry as a whole in 1977 and subsequent years.

Labor coefficients were computed by dividing employment in each occupation by an estimate of Unimation's 1982 output, $72 million. These coefficients were used to describe 1977 labor requirements and are shown in Table 2.11.

The Use of Robots

Capital Coefficients

The future use of robots in each sector is determined in the IEA database by: (1) an expansion coefficient which determines the investment in robots required to expand capacity by one unit (B matrix); and (2) a modernization coefficient which describes the annual investment in robots per unit of output in the absence of expansion (R matrix).

The U.S. stock of robots in 1980 can be valued at $218.4 million in 1979 prices—an estimated 2600 robots at a unit price of $84,000. There are no systematic data on the distribution of this stock among the different sectors of the economy. We based our estimate of this distribution on fragmentary information in trade journals, a survey estimating sales of robots to 13 manufacturing sectors in 1979 (Frost and Sullivan, 1979, p. 135), and a Delphi study conducted by the Society of Manufacturing Engineers estimating the share of robots purchased by specific industry groups (Smith and Wilson, 1983, p. 48). According to our decomposition, primary metal and metal fabricating sectors (IEA #36–41) accounted for 35%, and auto and farm equipment another 23% of the 1980 stock of robots. Almost 14% were held by producers of electrical equipment (#53–56), and 5.3% were used for aircraft production. The stock of robots per unit of sectoral output in 1980 was computed.

The future use of robots per unit of output was assumed to grow on a sector specific basis. The overall rate of growth of the stock required to produce a unit of output was assumed to be 15% a year between 1980 and 1990 under Scenario S2 and 25% under Scenario S3.

The first generation of industrial robots has been concentrated in the foundry and casting (IEA #36–41), Farm and Garden Machinery (IEA #43), Motor Vehicles (IEA #61), and Aircraft (IEA #62) industries. With the application of robots to assembly, materials handling, and machine tending, the sectoral distribution of installed robots should become more equal. Industries using small batch techniques (IEA #44–53) to produce metal parts, equipment, and machinery will vastly increase their use of robots for tool changing and materials handling. The use of robots per unit of output by sectors whose production processes are characterized primarily by assembly and packaging tasks [e.g., Household Appliances (IEA #53), Radio and TV (IEA #56), and Food and Kindred Products (IEA #13)] can also be expected to rise by larger than average increases in the future.

The sectoral composition of the stock of robots in 1980 is shown in Table 2.12. The last column in the table shows the corresponding composition of the much larger stock in 1990 and 2000 (to produce the same 1980 vector of output according to the sectoral stock to output coefficients projected for those years).

In this table the proportion of robots held by sectors IEA #36–41 in 1990 and 2000 is half the 1980 value, while Farm and Garden Machinery (IEA #43), Aircraft (IEA #62), and Motor Vehicles (IEA #61) each decline by 10%. The proportions held by all other industries increase by 50%, with the exception of Food Products (IEA #13), which rises by 300% in anticipation of the widespread application of robots to materials handling and packaging which play particularly important roles in this sector.

We assume that the greatest growth in the use of robots per unit of output will take place before 1990; in the following decade, the emphasis will instead be on the integration of robots into increasingly complex manufacturing sequences. We assumed that in each year starting in 1985, the capital coefficients governing the use of robots per unit increase in capacity (row 86 of the B matrix) would be the same as the average robot to output ratios projected for 1990. The purchase of robots per unit of sectoral output for the replacement of existing capac-

TABLE 2.12.   Distribution of Robots by Sector in 1980, 1990, and 2000

Code	Sector	1980	1990, 2000
12	Ordnance and Accessories	1.76%	2.64%
13	Food and Kindred Products	1.33	4.00
21	Household Furniture	.27	.40
22	Other Furniture and Fixtures	.27	.40
26	Chemicals and Selected Chemical Products	1.40	2.10
27	Plastics and Synthetic Materials	.50	.75
28	Drugs, Cleaning, and Toilet Preparations	.62	.93
29	Paints and Allied Products	.13	.20
31	Petroleum Refining and Allied Industries	1.76	2.64
34	Glass and Glass Products	.22	.33
35	Stone and Clay Products	1.11	1.66
36	Primary Iron and Steel Manufacturing	12.40	6.20
37	Primary Nonferrous Metals Manufacturing	8.10	4.00
38	Metal Containers	1.76	.80
39	Heating, Plumbing, and Structural Metal Products	4.60	2.30
40	Screw Machine Products and Stampings	3.54	1.77
41	Other Fabricated Metal Products	4.60	2.30
42	Engines and Turbines	.58	.87
43	Farm and Garden Machinery	3.10	2.80
44	Construction and Mining Machinery	.93	1.40
45	Materials handling Machinery and Equipment	.26	.40
46	Metalworking Machinery and Equipment	.62	.90
47	Special Industry Machinery and Equipment	.49	.74
48	General Industrial Machinery and Equipment	.88	1.32
49	Miscellaneous Machinery, except Electrical	.53	.80
50	Electronic Computing and Related Equipment	1.60	2.40
51	Office Equipment	.60	.90
52	Service Industry Machines	.60	.90
53	Electric Industrial Equipment and Apparatus	2.65	4.00
54	Household Appliances	4.73	7.10
55	Electric Lighting and Wiring Equipment	1.70	2.60
56	Radio, TV, and Communications Equipment	4.73	7.10
57	Electron Tubes	.22	.33
58	Semiconductors and Related Devices	.71	1.10
59	Electronic components, nec	1.20	1.80
60	Miscellaneous Electrical Machinery and Supplies	1.70	2.50
61	Motor Vehicles and Equipment	20.00	18.00
62	Aircraft and Parts	5.31	4.80
63	Other Transportation Equipment	1.50	2.25
64	Scientific and Controlling Instruments	.09	.14
65	Optical, Ophthalmical and Photographic Equipment	.09	.14
66	Miscellaneous Manufacturing	.22	.33
86	Robotics Manufacturing	.10	.15
	Total	100.00%	100.00%

ity—essentially the displacement of labor—in 1990 and 2000 was assumed to be the same as the average use of robots in the corresponding year.

Intermediate Input Coefficients

Because robots can be programmed to apply an identical coat of paint to each object, they can be expected to reduce requirements for paint per unit of output. It has been claimed that "in spray painting operations it is not uncommon to achieve a 10 to 30 percent savings in materials" (Teresko, 1979, p. 39). According to *The American Machinist* (Vaccari, 1982, p. 134), a Deere & Co. spokesperson claimed that the use of robots in the painting of tractors has reduced paint consumption by about 13%. Painting robots are most easily introduced into large-scale, standardized operations. Some workers operate automatic machinery for which robots are not applicable, while others use spray guns on small, specialized jobs that will not be robotized.

The Paint (IEA #29) coefficients for robot-using industries were projected according to the equation

$$a_{29j}^{t} = (1 - \alpha\beta^{t})a_{29j}^{77} \qquad (2\text{-}6)$$

where a_{29j}^{t} is the paint used per unit of output of industry j in time t, a_{29j}^{77} is the paint coefficient in 1977, β^{t} is the portion of painting tasks performed by robots in time t, and α is the percent savings in paint that follows from the use of robots. The savings in paint (α) was assumed to be 20%. We assumed that 15% of the painting tasks in 1990 and 25% in 2000 would be performed by robots under Scenario S2. Under Scenario S3 these figures are 25% and 40%, respectively. Table 2.13 summarizes these assumptions and shows that the new paint coefficients range from 97% of the 1977 coefficient in 1990 under Scenario S2, to 92% under S3 in 2000.

Labor Requirements

The growing use of robots will diminish the requirements for several categories of production workers per unit of output while increasing the need for specialized technicians. We assume that robots will be used for welding, painting, assembly, machine tending, and miscellaneous material handling. The first four operations affect Welders and Flame Cutters (LAB #43), Painters (LAB #42), Assemblers (LAB #39), and Other Operatives (semiskilled machine operators included in LAB #46). Materials-handling robots were assumed to replace Packagers and Wrappers (LAB #41) and Laborers (LAB #52).

TABLE 2.13. Impact of Robots on Paint Requirements per Unit of Output in 1990 and 2000[a]

	Scenario S2		Scenario S3	
	1990	2000	1990	2000
Proportion of paint saved (α)	.20	.20	.20	.20
Proportion of painting tasks performed by robots (β^t)	.15	.25	.25	.40
Paint coefficient as proportion of 1977 coefficient $(1 - \alpha\beta^t)$	.97	.95	.95	.92

[a]Parameters in this table are used in equation (2-6).

In this section we project the mix of operations for which robots will in the future be used in the different sectors of the economy and the rate of labor displacement per robot for each operation. Once a sector's stock of robots and output have been determined, the matrix of labor displacement per robot by occupation for each sector is used within the model to update its labor requirements per unit of output.

Projections of the use of robots in different applications in the auto industry and in all other manufacturing in the U.S. in 1990 have been made by Hunt and Hunt (1982, p. 42) and are shown in Table 2.14. We assume that Farm and Garden Machinery (IEA #43), Aircraft (IEA #62), and Other Transportation Equipment (IEA #63) will use the same share of robots in each application area as Hunt and Hunt project for Motor Vehicles (IEA #61). For most of the remaining sectors, materials-handling robots, primarily for packaging and in automated warehouse systems, were assumed to make up 10% of each sector's installed robots. In the food, chemicals, glass, and stone processing sectors (IEA #13, 26–29, 31, 34–35) the remaining share (90%) of the robot stock was allocated entirely to machine-tending applications. In primary metal processing (IEA #36, 37), 10% of the robots were assigned to welding, reducing those in machine-tending operations to 80%. The remaining metalworking sectors (IEA #12, 38–42, 44–49, 52) were assumed to use half their robots for machine tending—20% for welding, 20% for assembly, and 10% for materials-handling tasks. Finally, those industries specializing in assembling operations (IEA #53–59, 64, and 65) were assumed to use 30–60% of their robots for assembly.

Recent evidence from Japan suggests that among the most advanced robots currently in use, displacement rates of 2–4 workers

TABLE 2.14. Distribution of Projected U.S. Robot Population by Application in 1990

Application	Autos Range of estimates		All Other Manufacturing Range of estimate		Total Range of estimate	
	Low	High	Low	High	Low	High
Welding	3,200	4,100	5,000	10,000	8,700	14,100
	(21.3%)	(16.4%)	(15.7%)	(13.3%)	(17.4%)	(14.1%)
Assembly	4,200	8,800	5,000	15,000	9,200	23,800
	(28.0%)	(35.2%)	(14.3%)	(20.0%)	(18.4%)	(23.8%)
Painting	1,800	2,500	3,200	5,500	5,000	8,000
	(12.0%)	(10.0%)	(9.1%)	(7.3%)	(10.0%)	(8.0%)
Machine loading/ unloading	5,000	8,000	17,500	34,000	22,500	42,000
	(33.3%)	(32.0%)	(50.0%)	(45.3%)	(45.0%)	(42.0%)
Other	800	1,600	3,800	10,500	4,600	12,000
	(5.3%)	(6.4%)	(10.9%)	(14.0%)	(9.2%)	(12.1%)
Total	15,000	25,000	35,000	75,000	50,000	100,000
	(100.0%)	(100.0%)	(100.0%)	(100.0%)	(100.0%)	(100.0%)

Source: Hunt and Hunt, 1982.

58

per shift are possible. A study published by the Japan Industrial Robot Association (1982) includes the following examples:

> Arc welding system for two types of farm appliance components. . . . The number of workers required in this process has been reduced from 3 to 1 (p. 352).

> Automatic system to continuously operate five die cast machines with only one worker. . . . The operation of five die cast machines needed five workers—one for each machine before the robot was introduced. Now they can be satisfactorily run by only one person (p. 364).

> System for automatically piling up and cooling down aluminum ingots cast by a continuous casting machine. . . . Formerly, four workers had been needed to pile up ingots, but one operator is now able to attend to the entire line satisfactorily (p. 374).

> Full automatic mounting system for semiconductor chips. . . . One automated machine can perform work which, if carried out manually as before, would have required 6 workers (p. 234).

These examples appear to lie at the high end of the spectrum of displacement rates appearing in the literature. Displacement rates of 1.5 workers per shift in die casting and two workers per shift in press work are cited by Engelberger (1980, p. 145, 153). A Battelle Memorial Institute survey of five German factories (Ayres and Miller, 1983, p. 73) states that the average displacement per robot is 1.5 workers per shift. Based on 1.5 workers per robot and two-shift operations, we assumed that three workers are displaced per robot.

The literature also suggests that one robot technician will be required for every six robots per shift (Freedman, 1982, p. 34; Engelberger, 1980, p. 145). With two-shift operations, two robot technicians would be required for every 6 robots.

These rates were used to compute the number of workers displaced (or employed in the case of robot technicians) in each occupation per million dollars of a given sector's robot stock. Displacement (employment) coefficients are presented in Table 2.15 for three sectors. They indicate that Other Operatives (semiskilled machine operators included in LAB #46) are those most affected by robots in the Primary Iron and Steel sector, while Assemblers (LAB #39) are most affected in the production of Household Appliances. Direct displacement by robots in the Motor Vehicles industry is greatest for Assemblers, Machine Operators, and Welders (LAB #39, 46, and 43).

Most industry observers expect that because of their accuracy and

TABLE 2.15.   Direct Labor Displacement by Robots for Three Sectors (Workers per Million Dollars of Robots, 1979 Prices)

Code (Lab #)	Occupation	Primary Iron and Steel (IEA #36)	Household Appliances (IEA #54)	Motor Vehicles (IEA #61)
39	Assemblers	0	−14.30	−10.10
41	Packers and Wrappers	− 1.45	− 1.43	− .72
42	Painters	0	− 1.78	− 4.33
43	Welders and Flame Cutters	− 3.63	− 3.57	− 7.58
46	Other Machine Operatives	−28.50	−12.50	−11.90
47	Robot Technicians	3.97	3.97	3.97
52	Laborers	− 2.18	− 2.14	− 1.08

dependability, robots will displace inspectors and checkers as well. The Delphi forecasts conducted by the Society of Manufacturing Engineers (Smith and Wilson, 1982) concluded that 8% of inspectors will actually be displaced by robots in 1990, and 15% in 1995. Based on a survey of robot users, a Carnegie-Mellon University study concluded that Level 1 robots (similar to those on the market today) could do 13% of the jobs currently done by inspectors in metalworking industries (Ayres and Miller, 1981, p. 29). Using these figures as a rough guideline, we assumed that Inspectors (LAB #40) required per unit output in 1977 would fall by 8% by 1990 under Scenario S2, and 13% under S3. By 2000 we assumed a decline of 20% under S2, and 30% under S3.

In this chapter we have projected coefficients describing the future production of computers and associated technologies and the direct implications of their use in manufacturing. In the next chapter we take up the future use of computers in the automation of office operations.

REFERENCES

Allan, Roger. 1978. The 12th American machinist inventory of metalworking equipment, 1976–78. *American Machinist* 122, no. 12 (December):133–148.

————. 1984. Sensors in silicon. *High Technology* (September) 43–50.

Aron, Paul. 1982. Paul Aron Report No. 25. In Exploratory Workshop on the Social Impacts of Robotics. U.S. Congress. Office of Technology Assessment. Washington, D.C..

Ayres, Robert U. and Steven M. Miller. The Impacts of industrial robots. The Robotics Institute, Carnegie-Mellon University, Pittsburgh (unpublished).

————. 1983. *Robotics: applications and social implications.* Cambridge, Mass.: Ballinger Publishing Company.

Conigliaro, Laura. 1981. Robotics Presentation. New York: Bache Halsey Stuart Shields Inc.

Duke, John, and Horst Brand. 1981. Cyclical behavior of productivity in the machine tool industry. *Monthly Labor Review* 104, no. 11 (November):27–34.

Engelberger, Joseph. 1980. *Robotics in practice.* New York: American Management Association.

Freedman, Alix. 1982. Behind every successful robot is a technician. *New York Times* (October 17), section 12, p. 34.

Frost and Sullivan. 1979. The U.S. industrial robot market. No. 630. New York (January).

————. 1981. Machine tools programmable controls market. No. A826. New York (March).

————. 1982. Machine centers market in the U.S. No. A923. New York (May).

Hunt, H. Allan, and Timothy L. Hunt. 1982. *Robotics: human resource implications for Michigan.* Kalamazoo, Mich.: W.E. Upjohn Institute for Employment Research.

International Data Corporation. 1981. E.D.P. industry report: Review and forecast. 2 parts. Hamingham, Mass.

Iron Age. 1980. Computer sparks big savings in flame cutting. Vol. 19, no. 986 (February 25):7.

Japan Economic Journal. 1981. "Robot demand in non-mfg. sector will be slow. Vol. 223, no. 8 (December 22):116.

Japan Industrial Robot Association (JIRA). 1982. The specifications and applications of industrial robots in Japan 1982. Tokyo.

Kidd, John, and David E. Burnett. 1981. CAD/CAM interfaces. Technical Paper MS81–366. Dearborn, Mich.: Society of Manufacturing Engineers.

Levitan, Sar A., and Clifford M. Johnson. 1982. The future of work: does it belong to us or to the robots? *Monthly Labor Review* 105, no. 9 (September): 10–14.

Lund, Robert T. 1977. Numerically controlled machine tools and group technology: A study of the U.S. experience. Center for Policy Alternatives, Cambridge: M.I.T.

————. 1978. Integrated computer aided manufacturing: Social and economic impacts. Center for Policy Alternatives, Cambridge: M.I.T. (unpublished).

Marcus, Steven J. 1983. Robots' future taking shape. *New York Times* (August 18), D2 (unpublished).

National Machine Tool Builders Association. 1981. Economic handbook of the machine tool industry, 1981–82. Mc Lean, Va.

Real, Bernard. 1980. *The machine tool industry*. Paris: Organization for Economic Co-operation and Development.

Smith, Donald N., and Richard C. Wilson. 1982. *Industrial robots: A Delphi forecast of markets and technology*. Dearborn, Mich.: Society of Manufacturing Engineers.

Teresko, John. 1979. Control makers' challenge: Putting computers to work. *Industry Week*, 203, no.2 (October 15): 102–109.

U.S. Congress. Office of Technology Assessment. Technical options for conservation of metals. Washington, D.C.

U.S. Department of Commerce. Bureau of Economic Analysis. New structures and equipment by using industries, 1972: Detailed estimates and methodology. Washington, D.C. (September 1980).

————. Fixed reproducible wealth in the U.S., 1925–1979, Washington, D.C. (1982).

U.S. Department of Commerce. U.S. Industry and Trade Administration. A report on the U.S. semiconductor industry. Washington, D.C. (1979).

Vaccari, John. 1982. Robots that paint can create jobs. *American Machinist* 126, no. 1 (January): 131–134.

Zientara, Marguerite. 1983. Expenditures for personnel growing slower this year. *Computer World* 17, no. 27 (July 4):1, 4.

CHAPTER 3

The Automation of Office Work

The "Office of the Future" is the environment which will result from the widespread application of computer technology to daily office problems. . . . Much of the technology is in place but remains unintegrated; other parts . . . have yet to be developed in a cost-effective vehicle. Nevertheless, the next generation of office automation is at hand. The typewriters, copiers and file cabinets of today will go the way of the last generation's copy typists and records buildings and the previous generations' scriveners.[1]

During the 1950s and 1960s electronic data processing had a significant impact on the jobs of large numbers of clerical workers. The microprocessor-based office equipment of the 1970s extended the impact of electronic processing to a larger segment of white-collar workers, and the integrated electronic information systems being put in place today can be expected to affect virtually all white-collar workers. This chapter describes prospective developments in office automation and reports the technical coefficients that correspond to these assumptions. We will examine the changes in the input requirements of firms that produce office equipment, and describe the capital, intermediate, and labor requirements of sectors that use electronic office equipment and integrated systems.

Prior to the 1970s, the impact of the computer on office work was mainly to automate large routine and repetitive processing tasks. Separate data processing departments were created—in firms that could justify the purchase of a mainframe—to perform tasks that had been carried out manually by clerical workers in the back office such as billing, payroll, and certain bookkeeping functions. The physical flow of information to and from the centralized data processing department often resulted in bottlenecks that limited the advantages of electronic processing.

1. Frost and Sullivan, 1980a, pp. 16–17.

Advances in microelectronics during the 1970s reduced the bulk of the equipment and the cost of electronic processing and resulted in increased application to office functions. Office workers began to use electronic typewriters, word processors, optical character readers, and dictation equipment which increased the productivity of secretaries, typists, and other clerical workers who had been minimally affected by mainframe computer technology. More recently, microprocessor technology has also reached managers and professionals in the form of desktop computers.

The early emphasis of microprocessor-based office technology has been to increase the efficiency of office information systems already in place. Electronic or "intelligent" office machines have replaced conventional machines without altering the structure of the office. Information systems in the majority of offices are still based largely on the 8½ × 11 inch sheet of paper as an interface medium and continue to require manual intervention. According to a reviewer of office technology for *Fortune*, "Not all terminals have been designed to communicate with big corporate computers; almost none can interact easily with work stations of another brand nor can they always do so with work stations of the same brand" (Uttal, 1982). Microprocessor-based office equipment is now used in many more office processing tasks than mainframe computers; however, since a major function of an office is not only to process but also to communicate information, intelligent but isolated equipment has had only limited impacts.

The major trend in office technology today is to supplement, and in some instances replace, the paper information system with electronic storage and transmission. In recent electronic office systems, each component is capable of data and word processing and includes storage and a communications interface. Components are linked through high-speed networks that make it possible to share processing, access central storage facilities, and expedite the flow of information within an organization. Internal networks connect with common carrier networks to allow users on different local area networks to communicate. With the maturation of today's generation of applied information systems and decision support systems, organizations will be able to capture information once and subsequently process, transfer, store, and access it with a minimum of intervention.

Integrated systems have so far been implemented only in establishments that employ large numbers of white-collar workers such as large corporate offices. Start-up costs are significant, and firms are hesitant to invest because of the difficulty of estimating their future processing and communication requirements. The average price of complete systems installed for customers by Xerox, for example, is $270,000 (Uttal, 1982). According to a study by the Rand Corporation, "Of the estimated 3.5 million offices in the U.S. about 1.5 million are currently large enough for some sort of advanced information system" (Bikson and Gutek, 1983). This figure will increase as smaller and more flexible systems become available and start-up costs decline.

Falling hardware costs will hasten the adoption of advanced systems, and software development will remain the major bottleneck for the foreseeable future. New storage technologies, such as bubble and optical memories, will provide tremendous storage capacities at a fraction of today's cost for electronic storage. Some expect that 8K microprocessors capable of performing text editing will drop from $200 to $50 over the next 10 years (Burns, 1980). Another observer (Spinrad; 1982) anticipates that

> . . . individual chips will combine memory, logical processing, input-output interfaces, and, if appropriate, analog-to-digital conversion, allowing "intelligent" equipment functions to be dispersed to an unprecedented degree.

It will become necessary to establish standards to ensure the compatability necessary to integrate a variety of hardware and software components into operational short- and long-distance networks.

Advanced networks today are based on the ring principle that enables devices to communicate without a central processor. A local processor monitors a message stream for messages directed toward attached devices; the processor then extracts, formats, and transfers them to the appropriate destination. Since intelligence is distributed locally, these networks are faster, more reliable, and more efficient than point-to-point or star networks. As memory and processing costs continue to fall and advances in fiber optics provide increasing band widths, ring-type systems will offer significant cost advantages to offices installing them over the next few years. According to Spinrad (1982), "Local communication networks using optical fibers are likely to become common toward the end of the decade."

Vendors of office equipment are now selling local area networks, and the Bell system and switchboard companies are also active participants in this market with their automated PABX systems. PABX provides digital voice and data transmissions over existing telephone networks. According to Electronics Industry Association (1982), 30,000 offices will have PABX equipment for audio, data, and visual messages and for connecting interoffice work stations electronically by 1990.

Firms can be expected to invest in office systems to expand output and reduce unit costs. A widespread perception today is that the salaries of managers, professionals, and secretaries are rising while white-collar productivity is stagnant. According to one source, office salaries account for 50% of business costs, but office productivity rose by only 4% between 1960 and 1970 while factory productivity grew by 80% over the same period (Mortenson, 1982). Low investment in office capital is the reason most commonly cited for this discrepancy. Several authors observe that while white-collar employees work with only $2,000 in equipment, a factory worker today is backed up by $25,000 in machinery (Byron, 1981; Uttal, 1982). As the price of new office technology continues to fall, firms will replace manual office information systems, and new offices will be increasingly automated.

Frost and Sullivan (1980a) see the market for office systems expanding rapidly over the latter part of the 1980s. Other analysts believe that the indirect costs of planning, training, and supervision— activities that can cost as much as the technology itself—may delay investment in office systems (Uttal, 1982). New office procedures are often not directly related to the production of a firm's principal output, and the associated difficulty in measuring the productivity gains of new equipment is a deterrent to investment.

For the present study, we have elaborated two alternative scenarios about office automation. Scenario S2 assumes that firms will be slow to invest in integrated office systems and represents what now appears to be the lowest level of diffusion of integrated office technology that can be anticipated over the next 10 to 20 years. Scenario S3 represents, in our judgment, the maximum level of diffusion that is likely to occur through the year 2000. These scenarios will be described in more detail in the following sections.

The Production of Office Equipment

A shift in the composition of output produced by the Office Equipment sector (IEA #51) toward electronic text equipment will change its input requirements. In the early 1970s office equipment included conventional typewriters, mail machines, scales and balances, and duplicating machines. By the late 1970s, however, this sector began to use electronic components: electronic mail machines, scales and balances, and electronic text equipment were produced in addition to the conventional equipment. In the process, firms have necessarily increased their purchases of electronic components as reflected in the coefficient $a_{58,51}$ in the A matrix [i.e., the output of semiconductors (IEA #58) required to produce a unit of Office Equipment (IEA #51)].

We assume that all office equipment will be electronic by 1985. As a rough estimate of $a_{58,51}$ in 1985 we use the cost of a CPU board divided by the retail price of the word processor[2] and assume that this coefficient applies also to mail machines, scales, and balances. The coefficient is interpolated for years between 1977 and 1985 and over this period represents a weighted average of the input requirements for conventional and electronic equipment. The value of $a_{58,51}$ rises from 0.004 in 1977 to 0.05 by 1985 and remains at this level through 2000 under Scenarios S2 and S3. We assume that in all other ways the input structure of IEA #51 will remain unchanged after 1977.

The Use of Electronic Office Equipment

As offices within each sector of the economy invest in electronic office equipment and systems, other capital, intermediate and labor requirements will also be affected. A rise in the use of computers per unit of output, described in Chapter 2, will be the major change in capital requirements associated with the electronic office; however, demand for other office equipment will also be affected. Moreover, with increasing use of computers, demand for complementary inputs such as electricity and telecommunications and substitutes such as paper will be affected. The most important change will be in the white-collar labor necessary to perform many job tasks. This section describes the methods, data, and assumptions used to project changes in these technical coefficients with special emphasis on labor coefficients.

Capital Coefficients

The stock of office equipment, excluding office computers, per unit of sectoral output will increase through the mid 1980s but decline over the long run. Estimates of the annual market for electronic text equip-

---

2. Based on information provided by a technical supervisor at Hermes Business Products, Inc.

ment in the early 1980s range between \$2–7 billion (Marchant, 1979; Uttal, 1982; Frost and Sullivan, 1980a; Electronics Industries Association, 1982). Analysts project that by the mid 1980s intelligent work stations (produced by the computer sector, IEA #50) with word-processing capabilities will displace the electronic text equipment produced by IEA #51 (Frost and Sullivan, 1980a). Conventional typewriters will also be replaced by electronic text equipment or intelligent work stations and faster, cheaper photocopy machines will make duplicating machines obsolete over the next few years.

Investment in office equipment is governed by two of the coefficients in the IEA model. The capital coefficient, b_{51j}, represents the office equipment required to expand the capacity of the jth sector by one unit. The "modernization" coefficient, r_{51j}, describes purchases of new office equipment to replace obsolete equipment (or labor) in the absence of expansion.

Because of the increasing displacement by electronic text equipment of conventional office equipment, the expansion coefficients in row #51 of the B matrix are expressed in terms of two components:

$$b_{51j}^t = b_{aj}^t + b_{cj}^t \tag{3-1}$$

where b_{51j}^t is the value of office equipment required to increase output of sector j by one unit in year t, and by b_{aj}^t and by b_{cj}^t are the amounts of electronic and conventional office equipment, respectively, that will jointly be purchased in year t in order to increase the output of sector j by one unit. Coefficients were first estimated for 1977 (i.e., b_{aj}^{77} and b_{cj}^{77}) and then projected for future years.

We assumed that the average new office put in place in 1977 used the same mix of technologies as the average office already in place. To estimate b_{aj}^{77}, we first distributed the aggregate stock of electronic text equipment in 1977, valued at \$1.9 billion (Frost and Sullivan, 1980a), among sectors according to the percent of secretaries they employ. This distribution, shown in Table 3.1, allocates almost 70% of the stock to nine service sectors including Business Services, Education, Wholesale and Retail Trade, Finance, and Insurance. [Business Services includes the legal profession which is said to derive the largest direct gain from word processors (Uttal, 1982).] This stock is then divided by the sector's output in 1977 to produce the coefficient b_{aj}^{77}.

For b_{cj}^{77} we use the coefficient b_{51j} for 1972, a year predating electronic office equipment. Thus we assume an increased use of office equipment per unit of output between 1972 and 1977 with the entire increase consisting of electronic text equipment.

The aggregate stock of electronic text equipment per unit of gross output of the entire economy grew by an average of 37% annually between 1976 and 1980 (Frost and Sullivan, 1980a; U.S. Department of Labor, 1982). Under Scenario S2, we assume that this coefficient rises at an annual rate of 45% between 1977 and 1983 and falls to zero by 1985 by which time electronic text equipment is replaced by intelligent work stations. Under Scenario S3 we estimate only a 35% average annual increase between 1977 and 1983 for electronic text equipment as users move more quickly to intelligent work stations. We assume no change in the distribution of the stock of word processors across using sectors.

Under Scenario S2 we assume that investment in intelligent work stations will reduce the use of conventional typewriters to 25% of the 1977 value by 1985, based on estimates of the market for typewriters (Electronic Industries Association, 1982), and that duplicating machines will be obsolete. Typewriters and duplicating machines comprised 38 and 9%, respectively, of the capital goods portion of the output of IEA #51 in 1972 (U.S. Department of Commerce, 1980b). We assume that these proportions also reflect the approximate share of these machines in the total requirements for office equipment in which case b_{cj} falls to 62% of its 1977 value by 1985 under Scenario S2. Under Scenario S3 we assume that electronic text equipment and intelligent work stations will completely replace conventional typewriters by 1985; the coefficient for conventional equipment is 53% of its 1977 value. There are no further reductions in these coefficients after 1985 under either scenario.

With respect to modernization in the absence of expansion (R matrix), electronic replaces conventional office equipment through 1985, and both are replaced by integrated office systems produced by the Computer sector (IEA #50) after 1985. We estimate the replacement coefficients by first calculating the yearly change in the projected stock of electronic text equipment required to produce a 1977 level of gross output in each year from 1977 to 1985 (Frost and Sullivan, 1980a; U.S. Department of Labor, 1982). Since these projections are for a constant level of output, the yearly increment in this stock can be interpreted as total investment for modernization. As a second step, we allocate this total across sectors based on the percent of secretaries employed in each sector and divide by the sector's output in 1977.

TABLE 3.1.   Sectoral Distribution of Secretaries in 1978

Code	Sector	Percentage
1	Livestock and Livestock Products	0.1%
2	Other Agricultural Products	0.1
3	Forestry and Fishery Products	0.1
4	Agricultural, Forestry, and Fishery Services	0.2
5	Iron and Ferroalloy Ores Mining	0.0
6	Nonferrous Metal Ores Mining	0.0
7	Coal Mining	0.0
8	Crude Petroleum and Natural Gas	0.6
9	Stone and Clay Mining and Quarrying	0.0
10	Chemical and Fertilizer Mineral Mining	0.0
11	Construction	2.6
12	Ordnance and Accessories	0.2
13	Food and Kindred Products	1.0
14	Tobacco Manufactures	0.0
15	Broad and Narrow Fabrics, Yarn, and Thread Mills	0.3
16	Miscellaneous Textile Goods and Floor Coverings	0.1
17	Apparel	0.5
18	Miscellaneous Fabricated Textile Products	0.1
19	Lumber and Wood Products, except Containers	0.2
20	Wood Containers	0.0
21	Household Furniture	0.2
22	Other Furniture and Fixtures	0.1
23	Paper and Allied Products, except Containers	0.4
24	Paperboard Containers and Boxes	0.2
25	Printing and Publishing	1.8
26	Chemicals and Selected Chemical Products	0.5
27	Plastics and Synthetic Materials	0.2
28	Drugs, Cleaning, and Toilet Preparations	0.6
29	Paints and Allied Products	0.1
30	Petroleum Refining and Allied Industries	0.3
31	Rubber and Miscellaneous Plastic Products	0.6
32	Leather Tanning and Finishing	0.0
33	Footwear and Other Leather Products	0.1
34	Glass and Glass Products	0.1
35	Stone and Clay Products	0.4
36	Primary Iron and Steel Manufacturing	0.4
37	Primary Nonferrous Metals Manufacturing	0.3
38	Metal Containers	0.1
39	Heating, Plumbing, and Structural Metal Products	0.4
40	Screw Machine Products and Stampings	0.3
41	Other Fabricated Metal Products	0.4
42	Engines and Turbines	0.1
43	Farm and Garden Machinery	0.1
44	Construction and Mining Machinery	0.2

TABLE 3.1 *(cont'd).* Sectoral Distribution of Secretaries in 1978

Code	Sector	Percentage
45	Materials Handling Machinery and Equipment	0.1%
46	Metalworking Machinery and Equipment	0.3
47	Special Industry Machinery and Equipment	0.2
48	General Industrial Machinery and Equipment	0.3
49	Miscellaneous Machinery, except Electrical	0.2
50	Electronic Computing Equipment	0.4
51	Office, Computing, and Accounting Machines, except IEA #50	0.1
52	Service Industry Machines	0.3
53	Electric Industrial Equipment and Apparatus	0.5
54	Household Appliances	0.1
55	Electric Lighting and Wiring Equipment	0.2
56	Radio, TV, and Communications Equipment	0.7
57	Electron Tubes	0.1
58	Semiconductors and Related Devices	0.1
59	Electronic Components, nec	0.2
60	Miscellaneous Electrical Machinery and Supplies	0.2
61	Motor Vehicles and Equipment	0.6
62	Aircraft and Parts	0.6
63	Other Transportation Equipment	0.3
64	Scientific and Controlling Instruments	0.5
65	Optical, Ophthalmical, and Photographic Equipment	0.3
66	Miscellaneous Manufacturing	0.5
67	Transportation and Warehousing	2.0
68	Communications, except Radio and TV	1.2
69	Radio and TV Broadcasting	0.3
70	Electric, Gas, Water, and Sanitary Services	0.9
71	Wholesale Trade	7.5
72	Retail Trade	5.7
73	Finance	5.5
74	Insurance	6.5
75	Real Estate and Rental	2.1
76	Hotels, Personal and Repair Services except Auto	1.2
77	Business Services	15.1
78	Eating and Drinking Places	0.5
79	Automobile Repair Services	0.2
80	Amusements	0.8
81	Hospitals	5.0
82	Health Services, excluding Hospitals	5.4
83	Educational Services	11.6
84	Nonprofit Organizations	7.1
85	Government Enterprises	0.5
	Total	100.0

Source: U.S. Department of Labor, 1981.

Intermediate Coefficients

As firms move toward the electronic office, their use of certain intermediate inputs will also change. They will increase their requirements for network services supplied by the telecommunication sector and will also use more electricity. While not all observers agree, it is likely that purchases of paper per unit of sectoral output will be reduced. Since integrated office systems are only now being put in place, the magnitude of such changes is unclear. In this study we assume that intermediate coefficients for telecommunications, electricity, and paper remain at the 1977 values through 2000 for all scenarios.

Labor Coefficients

The magnitude of the decline in labor coefficients for a particular occupation due to OA will depend on a variety of factors. Each occupation encompasses several tasks, and changes in labor coefficients will depend on the amount of time that a worker spends performing a particular task and the amount of automatic equipment applied to that task. Another consideration is the amount of the office worker's time that can be saved in performing a particular task by the use of automatic equipment. "Listening" typewriters, for example, can save 100% of the time required to produce a typewritten document while electronic typewriters may save only 50% of typing time. Also pertinent is the percent of workers of a particular occupation and sector that actually use the new technology in a given year. Finally, an increase in demand for certain office activities may partially offset labor savings from new technology. Equation (3-2) shows how labor coefficients can be projected to take each of these factors into account:

$$e^t_{kj} = \sum_{f=1}^{F} w_{fkj} \, [\mu^t_{fkj} + (1 - \mu^t_{fkj})(1 - \gamma^t_{fkj})(1 + \rho^t_{fkj})] e_{kj} \qquad (3\text{-}2)$$

where the variables are defined as follows:

e^t_{kj} Number of workers of occupation k per unit of output of sector j in year t.

γ_{fkj} Proportion of time saved by the new technology relative to the old technology for workers of occupation k in sector j performing task f ($f = 1, \ldots, F$).

μ^t_{fkj} Proportion of workers in occupation k in sector j performing task f in year t who are not affected by the new technology.

ρ^t_{fkj} Increase in demand for task f performed by workers of occupation k per unit of output of sector j in year t.

w_{fkj} Proportion of the time workers of occupation k in sector j spent in performing task f in the base year, just prior to the change in technology, where

$$\sum_{f=1}^{F} w_{fkj} = 1$$

e_{kj} Number of workers of occupation k per unit of output of sector j in the base year, just prior to the change in technology.

Equation (3-2) adjusts a base-year coefficient to reflect the diffusion of a time-saving technology and an increase in demand for certain labor functions. The expression $(1 - \gamma^t_{fkj})(1 + \rho^t_{fkj})e_{kj}$ shows the amount of time necessary to perform a particular task with the new equipment. To process 200% more text with a technology that saves 80% of the time required with the old technology, for example, requires 60% of the time that would have been required for the text-processing task with the old technology, $(1 - 0.8)(1 + 2) = 0.6$. Clearly an increase in demand for text processing moderates the amount of time saved by the new technology.

The parameter μ_{fkj} preserves the old labor coefficient for workers of occupation k in sector j who do not work with a new technology that affects task f. If $\mu^t_{fkj} = 0.75$ (i.e., only 25% of the workers of occupation k in sector j use word processors in the above example), then the labor required for text processing per unit of output of sector j in year t, as a proportion of the labor required in the base year, is $0.75 + 0.25(0.6) = 0.9$.

The parameter w_{fkj} weights each task performed by its share of total labor time. If secretaries, for example, spend only 20% of their total labor time processing text, and if office technology affects no other secretarial tasks, then (continuing the example above), the new labor coefficient for secretaries would be $0.8(1.0) + 0.2(0.9) = 0.98\ e_{kj}$.

In the absence of sufficiently detailed information on the breakdown of labor tasks we have simplified the parameters in equation (3-2). For most occupations, we distinguish only between those tasks that can be automated and those that cannot, and the parameter w_{kj} represents the proportion of time of workers of occupation k in sector j spent on tasks that can be automated. The proportion of time saved by the automatic equipment on the average in affected tasks is γ_{kj}, and μ_{kj} represents the proportion of workers not affected by automatic equipment (all in year t). We also assume that $\rho_{fkj} = 0$ for all tasks, occupations, and sectors. Equation (3-2') incorporates these modifications of equation (3-2):

$$e_{kj}^t = [w_{kj}^t(\mu_{kj}^t + (1 - \mu_{kj}^t)(1 - \gamma_{kj}^t)) + (1 - w_{kj}^t)]e_{kj} \qquad (3\text{-}2')$$

Table 3.2 contains the labor coefficients for each scenario as proportions of the coefficients in 1977, based on equation (3-2'). Since the IEA occupational classification is in some cases more aggregated than the detail in which these computations were carried out, for certain occupations (LAB #19, 20, 24), the proportions in Table 3.2 are weighted averages of the proportions for more detailed occupations. For clerical workers these proportions apply to all IEA sectors, since we assume that tasks performed by white-collar workers in a particular occupation are relatively homogeneous across industries and that new office technology is used by the same share of workers in an occupation for all industries. The assumptions for managers and salesworkers in different sectors are discussed in the text that follows.

The remainder of this section describes the information and assumptions that underlie the parameters used to calculate the proportions in Table 3.2. The discussion is organized by occupation, and the parameters for each of eight occupational categories (LAB #17–24) are summarized in Tables 3.3–3.10. Where possible, parameter values are based on the findings of case studies of the direct impact of office technology on particular occupations. Future studies will hopefully provide more systematic and detailed information on these parameters.

Managers (LAB #17)

It has been observed that for office automation to achieve its potential in reducing labor costs, it will be necessary for manufacturers to "reach beyond the secretary to managers and professionals who account for 80% of white collar salaries" (Uttal, 1982). Desktop computers integrated into networks can save a significant amount of time that managers spend processing information. With direct access to external and internal data banks, managers can prepare market studies, forecast competition, and develop pricing strategies in a few hours—activities that once took several months of work. Moreover, keyboard access to electronic files can reduce the amount of time spent looking for information, and graphics software enables managers to digest information quickly from computer printouts.

In addition to providing managers with local processing power, integrated systems can save time in a variety of communication activi-

TABLE 3.2. Labor Coefficients in 1990 and 2000 as Proportions of Labor Coefficients in 1977[a]

	Scenario S2		Scenario S3	
	1990	2000	1990	2000
Managers (LAB #17) all sectors except IEA # 76, 78, 79, 80	.99	.88	.84	.50
Sales Workers (LAB #18) sectors IEA #72, 78, 79, 80	.98	.96	.94	.89
All other sectors	.99	.95	.84	.75
Stenographers, Typists, and Secretaries (LAB # 19)	.85	.76	.65	.45
Office Machine Operators (LAB #20)	.45	.15	.28	0.00
Bank Tellers (LAB #21)	.80	.60	.60	.36
Telephone Operators (LAB #22)	.88	.81	.63	.50
Cashiers (LAB #23)	.98	.95	.93	.85
Other Clerical Workers (LAB #24)	.88	.74	.68	.59

[a]All entries computed with equation (3-2′) except the fourth row (LAB #19) which was computed with equation (3-2).

ties. Electronic mail can expedite dissemination of memos within an organization and correspondence between firms. Systems that record telephone messages digitally (by computer) and forward them to others within a company can reduce time spent trying to make contact with others. Computerized scheduling of meetings minimizes the need for individual contacts, and teleconferencing can reduce travel time associated with meetings in different locations.

Beyond the time saved in managerial activities, integrated systems may also eliminate certain middle manager positions entirely. According to *Business Week* (1983b), the role of middle managers since World War II has been to collect, analyze, and interpret information and pass it on to executives. "As more top managers see that much of the information once gathered by middle managers can be obtained faster, less expensively, and more thoroughly by computers, they have begun to view many middle managers as 'redundant.'" Specialized software programs that can replace certain middle management tasks include computerized inventory control, production scheduling, and allocation planning for limited resources. In addition, as integrated office systems reduce the number of clerical and other white-collar workers, fewer managers will be needed to supervise them.

The parameters used to project the coefficients governing the

TABLE 3.3.   Parameters that Determine Labor Coefficients for Managers (LAB #17) in 1990 and 2000[a]

	Scenario S2		Scenario S3	
Parameters	1990	2000	1990	2000
All sectors except IEA #76, 78, 79, 80				
Proportion of managers not affected by new technology (μ_{17j})	.90	.50	.35	.00
Proportion of managers' time spent in tasks affected by new office technology (w_{17j})	.15	.25	.25	.50
Proportion of managers' time saved by new technology relative to old (γ_{17j})	1.00	1.00	1.00	1.00

[a]Inserting these parameters in equation (3-2′) results in the proportions in the first row of Table 3.2.

demand for managers in 1990 and 2000 are shown in Table 3.3. The Electronic Industries Association estimates that 3% of all managers and professionals used desktop computers in 1982, and International Data Corporation (IDC) estimates that this share will rise to 65% by 1990 (Electronic Industries Association, 1982). For Scenario S2 we assume that 10% of all managers in each industry will use desktop computers or managerial work stations by 1990 (μ_{17j} = 0.90). By 2000 we assume that this share will be at least 50%. For Scenario S3 we use the IDC estimate that 65% of managers will use work stations by 1990. By 2000 we assume that all managers use work stations under this scenario.

The values of the parameter w_{17j}, the percent of a manager's time spent in tasks that can be automated, are based on a survey of managerial and professional productivity by management consultants Booz Allen and Hamilton. They found that middle managers on average spend 52% of total work time at meetings, 12% creating documents, and 16% analyzing and reading. The 20% of work hours that remain are spent in activities such as waiting for meetings, organizing information, expediting and assigning tasks, as well as scheduling, searching for information, filing, copying, transcribing, and other clerical-type activities. The study concludes that 15% of a manager's time can be saved by electronic office systems over the next five years (*Business Week*, 1983a). Based on these findings, for Scenario S2 we assume that by 1990 managers with executive work stations can save 100% of their labor time (γ = 1.00) in the 15% of their labor tasks that are mainly clerical (w = 0.15). As specialized managerial software is designed for integrated systems under Scenario S3, we assume that 25% of all managerial activities may be fully automated by 1990, and at least this amount will be automated by 2000 even under Scenario S2. By 2000 we assume that integrated systems may fully automate 50% of managerial activities under Scenario S3.

These changes in the labor coefficients for managers apply to all sectors except Hotels (IEA #76), Eating and Drinking Places (IEA #78), Automobile Repair (IEA #79), and Amusements (IEA #80). A large share of the managers in these retail sectors are proprietors or managers of single-manager establishments on whom office technology may have a negligible effect.

Sales Workers (LAB #18)

The sales staff in most sectors seeks out clients, travels, provides potential buyers with information, and processes paperwork. By contrast, in retail establishments, which employ over 50% of all sales workers, the job requires no travel, limited sales promotion, and much more time processing a greater volume of transactions. Electronic office technology will have a different effect on these two categories of sales workers.

The effects of automation on labor requirements for sales workers in retail establishments will be similar to that for cashiers. While sales persons in retail stores generally interact with customers more than cashiers, most of their time is devoted to processing transactions. Electronic technology in retail sales work reduces the time required to process transactions and record inventory information at check-out points. Point-of-sales terminals can raise productivity of sales clerks by 10% according to Maeda (1981). Another study of the impact of automated checkout equipment on cashiers notes a similar gain; labor requirements to process the same volume of transactions were reduced between 10 and 15% (U.S. Department of Labor, 1979).

The parameters used to project the coefficients for retail sales workers, shown in Table 3.4, are based on these studies and other assumptions. Under Scenario S2, we assume that point-of-sales terminals save 10% of the time required to process transactions and record inventory information with conventional cash registers. For Scenario S3 we assume that this equipment may save as much as 15% of this time.

In addition, for Scenario S2 we assume that 25% of sales workers will use point-of-sales terminals by 1990 and that this share will rise to 50% by 2000. Under Scenario S3 we assume that 50% of all retail sales workers may use automated checkout equipment by 1990 and that all sales workers may be affected by the year 2000. These are the same

TABLE 3.4.   Parameters That Determine Labor Coefficients for Sales Workers (LAB # 18) in 1990 and 2000[a]

Parameters	Scenario S2		Scenario S3	
	1990	2000	1990	2000
a. Retail Sectors (IEA #72, 78, 79, 80)				
Proportion of sales workers not affected by new office technology (μ_{18j})	.75	.50	.50	.00
Proportion of sales worker time spent in tasks affected by new office technology (w_{18j})	.75	.75	.75	.75
Proportion of time saved by new technology relative to old (γ_{18j})	.10	.10	.15	.15
b. All Other Sectors				
Proportion of sales workers not affected by new office technology (μ_{18j})	.90	.50	.35	.00
Proportion of sales worker time spent in tasks affected by new office technology (w_{18j})	.50	.50	.50	.50
Proportion of time saved by new technology relative to old (γ_{18j})	.20	.20	.50	.50

[a]Inserting these parameters in equation (3-2′) results in the proportions in rows 2 and 3 of Table 3.2.

parameters used below for cashiers; however, since retail sales workers have other tasks besides processing and recording transactions, we assume that unlike cashiers only 75% of a sales worker's time is affected by automated equipment. The remaining 25% of a sales worker's work time is spent assisting customers and keeping store merchandise in order, activities that will be unaffected by electronic technology.

While electronic technology will affect only the transaction processing task of sales workers in retail establishments, sales workers in most industries will be affected in a variety of ways. Direct access to external computerized data banks from government and private sources will assist sales people in identifying markets. Mobile telephones, voice message systems, and portable terminals will provide access to cost estimates, product supply, and delivery dates while also minimizing visits to field offices. Moreover, portable terminals will make it possible to process transactions more quickly.

Parameter projections for nonretail sales workers are shown in the bottom portion of Table 3.4. Each scenario assumes that 50% of a sales worker's time will be affected by office automation. This ratio, higher than that for managers and lower than that for secretaries, is based on the assumption that nonretail sales workers spend at least half their work time in face-to-face interaction with customers. The amount of time saved by the technology in those tasks that are affected is based on an estimate by vendors that sales persons can reduce selling time by 50% when they use office computer facilities and communication networks (*Business Week*, 1983a). We use this estimate for Scenario S3; for Scenario S2 we assume that office systems will save at least 20% of the time spent in affected tasks. Finally, we assume that the share of nonretail sales workers that use automated systems in a given year is the same as that reported for managers.

Secretaries, Typists, and Stenographers (LAB #19)

As a communications intermediary among managers, professionals, and others both inside and outside an organization, a secretary performs a variety of tasks that are affected by electronic office technology. At present, office technology has had its greatest impact on typing. Studies show that approximately 500,000 or 11% of all secretaries used word-processing equipment in 1981 (Walsh, 1982). This equipment produces remarkable gains in productivity when it is properly selected and used. According to one study (Administrative Manager, 1978),

> . . . typical individual secretaries ostensibly type 60 words per minute. Actually, when all the error white-outs and page-length remakes are figured in, they only type three or four words per minute. Typing specialists with automated equipment and good supervision can achieve from 15 to 30 words per minute, again taking into account all the setting up, referencing, and button-pushing. This represents a speed-up of from 500 to 1,000 percent.

Several studies show that the time saved by word-processing equipment can reduce labor requirements up to 50%. One review of a large multiservice law firm notes reductions of 50% in the number of typists required per constant dollar of revenue (Murphree, 1982). Another study cites several cases in which word-processor installations have reduced office staffs by one third to one half (Dowing, 1980). In one research organization word-processing equipment reduced average number of days to prepare a report by 20%, effectively reducing labor requirements by 20% (Karon, 1982).

While an increase in demand by firms for processed text will offset a decline in labor requirements, this effect will be temporary in most cases. One study of a word-processing installation notes that a common occurrence with word processors is that a lot of hidden work appears that has never been done before due to a lack of secretarial support (EDP Analyzer, 1980). A properly managed word-processing installation, however, will allow only those increases in typed material that effectively contribute to the total output of the firm. Thus, although employment may not immediately contract as word processors are installed, labor requirements per unit of output will still fall as output rises.

Although word processing will continue to provide significant gains in the productivity of typists, voice input technology will completely automate the typing task. Computer-based interpretation of voice data is an extension of dictation systems that bypasses the transcription task of secretaries. According to Gould et al. (1982) at the IBM research center,

> . . . with a listening typewriter, an author could dictate a letter, memo or report. What he or she says would be automatically recognized and displayed in front of him or her. A listening typewriter would combine the best features of dictating (rapid human output) and the best features of writing (visual record/easy editing). No human typist would be required and no delay would occur between the time an author creates a letter and when he or she gets it back in typed form.

Several voice data entry products are presently available for single-word application such as inventory, quality control, and credit authorization. However, according to researchers at IBM, "machine recognition of speech uttered by any person may or may not be achieved early in the next century" (Gould et al., 1982). Listening typewriters being tested today have a limited ability to discern word segmentation in normal speech patterns. When voice input technology does become available for everyday office use, virtually all white-collar workers will be affected. This application, however, is still in the developmental stage, and we make no attempt to incorporate its impacts on labor requirements. Rather, we consider only the continued diffusion of word-processing facilities in the form first of stand-alone equipment and then of integrated work stations.

Word-processing facilities will have their greatest impact on secretaries who type full time, approximately 22% of the workers in LAB #19 (U.S. Department of Labor, 1981). We assume that 100% of a typist's time will be affected by word processing that saves 80% of the time required with conventional typewriters. This represents a 500% increase in productivity, the lower bound on the productivity increase of word processing cited above (*Administrative Management*, 1978).

Furthermore, we project that at least 40% (Scenario S2) and as many as 70% (Scenario S3) of all typists will use word-processing facilities by 1990. These estimates are based on the fact that 11% of all secretaries used word-processing equipment in 1980 (Uttal, 1982) and the expectation that the real price of text-editing equipment will continue to fall over the 1980s. By 2000 we assume that at least 70% (Scenario S2) of all typists will have word-processing facilities, and under Scenario S3 we assume that all typists will use them. These parameters are shown under section b of Table 3.5.

Word-processing facilities will have much more moderate effects on secretaries who spend only part of their time typing. Secretaries not

TABLE 3.5. Parameters That Determine Labor Coefficients for Secretaries and Typists in 1990 and 2000[a]

	Scenario S2		Scenario S3	
Parameters	1990	2000	1990	2000
a. Secretaries				
Proportion of secretaries not affected by word processing ($\mu_{1,19a,j}$)	.60	.30	.30	.00
Proportion of secretary time spent in tasks affected by word processing ($w_{1,19a,j}$)	.20	.20	.20	.20
Proportion of time saved by word processing relative to conventional typing ($\gamma_{1,19a,j}$)	.80	.80	.80	.80
Proportion of secretaries affected by other office technology ($\mu_{2,19a,j}$)	.90	.50	.35	.00
Proportion of secretary time affected by other office technology ($w_{2,19a,j}$)	.45	.45	.45	.45
Proportion of time saved by new technology relative to old ($\gamma_{2,19a,j}$)	.25	.25	.75	.75
b. Typists				
Proportion of typists not affected by word processing ($\mu_{19b,j}$)	.60	.30	.30	.00
Proportion of typist time spent in tasks affected by word processing ($w_{19b,j}$)	1.00	1.00	1.00	1.00
Proportion of time saved by word processing ($\gamma_{19b,j}$)	.80	.80	.80	.80

[a]Taking a weighted average of the two proportions defined by inserting the parameters for a into equation (3-2) and the parameters for b into equation (3-2') results in the proportions in row 4 of Table 3.2. As weights we use secretaries and typists as a share of LAB #19 in 1978 as reported in U.S. Department of Labor (1981).

classified as full-time typists comprise 76% of all workers in LAB #19 (U.S. Department of Labor, 1981). For them, we use the same parameters as for full-time typists except for the weight of the typing task in total secretary work time. Studies show that on average secretaries spend approximately 20% of total work time typing (Green, 1982; Walsh, 1982).

Although word processing will affect only a small share of secretaries' work time, integrated office systems will affect many other secretarial tasks depending upon the facilities available at manager and professional work stations. At the limit, a manager who can access information from an electronic file, dictate a memo into a desktop computer, edit it verbally, and distribute and file it electronically will require little secretarial assistance. For these reasons, we assume that if a certain proportion of managers is connected to a network in year *t*, the network will extend to the same proportion of secretaries in that year.

Nonetheless, the share of secretarial time affected by office automation will be significantly greater than that of managers at least for the near future. Secretaries spend approximately 45% of their work time filing, mailing, making photocopies, delivering messages, and waiting for work (Green, 1982). Offices with secretarial work stations connected to electronic filing cabinets, electronic mail systems, and local printers will save time in all these areas. In each scenario we assume that 45% of all secretarial time will be affected by office automation other than electronic text processing.

The proportion of time saved will depend on the share of offices and office workers connected to the network. As long as some offices or clients are not connected electronically to others, interoffice communication will require that secretaries handle paperwork—and even when all offices are automated, these tasks will still consume at least some secretarial time. We assume that office systems will save at least 25% of the time spent in affected activities (Scenario S2) and that this equipment may save as much as 75% of this time (Scenario S3).

Microprocessor-based office technology will continue to replace full-time stenographers who now comprise about 2% of LAB #19 and whose work will be completely automated by 1990. Stenography has been a declining occupation since the 1960s when IBM first marketed its magnetic belt dictation unit. In addition to desktop and portable units available today, central dictation systems based on microprocessor technology serve many users, require fewer dictation units, and can be accessed over the telephones. One study shows that 60–70% of all organizations have some form of dictation equipment but that only one third of all people who originate typewritten work today use dictation machines (Frost and Sullivan, 1982). As offices continue to increase efficiency, utilization of dictation equipment will increase. Each scenario assumes that stenographers are completely replaced by 1990.

Office Machine Operators (LAB #20)

Office Machine Operators include clerical workers who operate conventional office equipment such as tabulating, calculating, bookkeeping, billing, keypunch machines, and those who operate peripheral computer equipment. Operators of conventional equipment represented 66% of all office machine operators in 1970; by 1978 this share dropped to 44%. An increase in the number of workers who operate peripheral computer equipment over the 1970s more than compensated for the decline in operators of conventional equipment, and the total number of operators grew by over 30% between 1970 and 1978 (U.S. Department of Labor, 1981).

Computer technology will soon eliminate all operators of conventional office machines, including keypunch operators. Small businesses that can now afford computers will replace conventional equipment, and data typists using video display terminals will continue to replace keypunch operators over the short run. We assume that the labor coefficient for operators of conventional equipment will fall to zero by 1990 in both scenarios.

The labor coefficient for operators of peripheral equipment such as data typists will fall less dramatically over the next two decades. As firms attempt to raise office productivity by increasing the amount of information captured electronically, they will invest in automated equipment such as optical readers (OCRs) and electronic cash registers that record information at the point of transactions. OCRs (machines that tranform visual input into numeric computer codes) can read 75–120 characters per second, while a fast keyboard operator can achieve at best 7. Until now, OCRs have been used mainly to read utility payments and charge card slips and to scan the 80% of first-class mail that is typewritten (Brody, 1983). Recent advances which have made OCR's much more reliable and reduced the cost to approximately $7,000 will accelerate the replacement of data typists.

The labor coefficient for other types of peripheral computer operators will also decline in the future. As distributed electronic processing replaces mainframe installations, workers who load and change tapes and remove output from high-speed printers at these facilities will also be displaced. We assume that mainframe attendants and data typists

TABLE 3.6. Parameters That Determine Labor Coefficients for Office Machine Operators in 1990 and 2000[a]

	Scenario S2		Scenario S3	
Operators of peripheral computer equipment	1990	2000	1990	2000
Proportion of operators not affected by new office technology ($\mu_{20a,j}$)	0.80	0.15	0.50	.00
Proportion of operator time spent in tasks affected by new office technology ($w_{20a,j}$)	1.00	1.00	1.00	1.00
Proportion of time saved by new technology relative to old ($\gamma_{20a,j}$)	1.00	1.00	1.00	1.00

[a]Inserting these parameters in equation (3-2′) and multiplying by the share of LAB #20 who operate peripheral computer equipment as reported in U.S. Department of Labor (1981) results in proportions in row 5 of Table 3.2.

can be completely eliminated. Under Scenario S2, 20% of these workers will be displaced by 1990, and 80% by 2000. Scenario S3 accelerates this displacement to 50% by 1990, and 100% by 2000. These assumptions are summarized in Table 3.6.

Bank Tellers (LAB #21)

> A human teller can handle up to 200 transactions a day, works 30 hours a week, gets a salary anywhere from $8000 to 20,000 a year plus fringe benefits, gets coffee breaks, a vacation and sick time. . . . In contrast, an automated teller can handle 2000 transactions a day, works 168 hours a week, costs about $22,000 a year to run and does not take coffee breaks or vacations (Bennett, 1983).

Automated transaction machines (ATMs), having achieved widespread acceptance by the American public, will have significant impacts on the labor requirements for human bank tellers. According to a report by BLS economists, the effectiveness of these machines in reducing waiting lines and extending banking hours induced banks to install 1900 ATMs by 1980 (Brand and Duke, 1982). The average number of transactions per month on ATMs grew by 250% between 1976 to 1980. One bank reports that two ATM's can perform the work of three human tellers (*Bank Systems and Equipment*, 1983). According to Brand and Duke (1982), larger banks can more easily justify the purchase of ATMs while for many small and medium-sized banks, the relatively high fixed costs of equipment are not offset by the savings in labor costs at current volumes of business—a factor that tends to retard the diffusion of the devices.

Future labor coefficients for bank tellers depend on several assumptions. Based on discussion with an official in the transactions processing department of Citicorp Bank, we assume that 80% of the transactions performed by bank tellers are routine and can easily be replicated by ATMs. We further assume that by 1990 at least half (Scenario S2), but perhaps all (Scenario S3), large banks will install ATMs. Large banks with assets in excess of $500 million employ almost 50% of all bank employees (Frost and Sullivan, 1980b). If large banks employ the same share of bank tellers, then at least 25% (Scenario S2) but as many as 50% (Scenario S3), of bank tellers will be affected by 1990. By 2000 at least all large banks will install ATMs (Scenario S2) while under Scenario S3 all medium-sized banks will follow suit. Since medium banks, with assets between 50 and $500 million, employ 31% of all bank employees, we assume that 80% of all bank tellers may use ATMs by 2000 (Scenario S3). Table 3.7 summarizes these assumptions.

Telephone Operators (LAB #22)

The continuous advance in the technology for switching telephones and recording information has steadily reduced the number of operators required to support a given number of telephones. In 1910, the Bell system employed 100,000 operators to service seven million telephones. By 1970, the system provided services to 98 million telephones with only 166,000 telephone operators (Scott, 1982). Several technological innovations account for this remarkable gain in productivity. The development of crossbar switches in the 1940s increased network capacity and in part made possible the introduction of direct distance dialing in 1951 that greatly reduced the number of operator-

TABLE 3.7. Parameters That Determine Labor Coefficients for Bank Tellers in 1990 and 2000[a]

Parameters	Scenario S2		Scenario S3	
	1990	2000	1990	2000
Proportion of bank tellers not affected by automation ($\mu_{21,73}$)	0.75	0.50	0.50	0.20
Proportion of bank teller time spent in tasks affected by automation ($w_{21,73}$)	0.80	0.80	0.80	0.80
Proportion of time saved by new technology relative to old ($\gamma_{21,73}$)	1.00	1.00	1.00	1.00

[a]Inserting these parameters in equation (3-2′) results in coefficients in row 6 of Table 3.2.

assisted calls. More recently, computers have been used to automate equipment through stored program control. Electronic switching systems (ESS), for example, use stored program control to switch telephone calls. Although ESS has its greatest impact on installers and maintenance workers, it is also changing many of the duties of operators through electronic consoles that automate most of the switching and billing tasks on operator-assisted long distance calls. In 1979 almost 75% of all telephones were serviced by these consoles which are reported to increase operator efficiency by 25% (U.S. Department of Labor, 1979). Other computer-based applications that will automate certain types of operator tasks are computer-assembled voice intercept devices and systems that automate coin telephones.

Future labor requirements for operators will depend on the rate at which computer applications become available to certain types of telephone operators. Since the telecommunication sector is likely to remain a rapid innovator, we assume that at least 50% (Scenario S2), but as many as 75% (Scenario S3), of the operators will be affected by 1990. By 2000 we assume that at least 75% (Scenario S2), but perhaps all operators (Scenario S3), will be affected by new computer software. In both scenarios, computer applications are assumed to affect 100% of an operator's tasks. As an estimate of the time that computers save in operators' tasks under Scenario S2, we use the 25% efficiency gain of electronic consoles cited by the Department of Labor. Under Scenario S3, we assume that this parameter may be as large as 50%. These parameters are shown in Table 3.8.

Cashiers (IEA #23)

Cashiers, the third largest clerical occupation after secretaries and bookkeepers, accounted for almost 1.5 million workers or 1.5% of the entire labor force in 1978. This was almost 50% greater than total employment of cashiers in 1970. The majority of cashiers, 62%, are employed in Retail Trade, 18% are employed in Eating and Drinking Places, and the remaining cashiers are scattered throughout the economy (U.S. Department of Labor, 1981).

The diffusion of computerized checkout systems will have a significant impact on cashiers. The most common type of computerized checkout machines today are supermarket scanners which transmit the universal product code of each purchase to a computer that is programmed to record the description and price of an item, add the tax, and print a receipt. According to one study of 38 supermarkets in the Washington area that installed scanner equipment, "a fully scanner

TABLE 3.8.   Parameters That Determine Labor Coefficients for Telephone Operators in 1990 and 2000[a]

Parameters	Scenario S2		Scenario S3	
	1990	2000	1990	2000
Proportion of operators not affected by automation (μ_{22j})	.50	.25	.25	0.00
Proportion of operator time spent in tasks affected by automation (w_{22j})	1.00	1.00	1.00	1.00
Proportion of time saved by new technology relative to old (γ_{22j})	.25	.25	.50	.50

[a]Inserting these parameters into equation (3-2′) results in proportions in row 7 of Table 3.2.

equipped supermarket was found to have a 5% lower labor requirement than an unautomated store with the same volume" (Gilchrist and Shenkin, 1982). Another survey cited by the BLS finds that "an electronic front end permits a 30% increase in operator ringing speed and a possible overall 10 to 15% reduction in unit labor requirements for cashiers and baggers" (U.S. Department of Labor, 1979b).

In addition to supermarket scanners, other forms of electronic checkout equipment will save the time of cashiers in nonfood retail stores. Point-of-sales terminals that read magnetically encoded vendor market merchandise tickets save data entry time of cashiers in large department, apparel, and discount stores. Moreover, electronic cash registers that perform credit-card authorization tasks further reduce the unit labor requirement for cashiers.

We assume that 100% of a cashier's work time will be affected by automated checkout equipment. Based on the study cited by BLS, we further assume that automated equipment saves 10% of the checkout time required for a given volume of transactions under Scenario S2, and that for Scenario S3 this equipment may save 15% of a cashier's time. Since all large food stores are expected to install scanner equipment by 1990 (Gilchrist and Shenkin, 1979), and large supermarkets employ about 10% of all cashiers in the Retail Trade sector (U.S. Department of Commerce, 1980a), we estimate that at least 25% of all cashiers (Scenario S2) will use automated equipment by 1990 assuming full automation of large supermarkets and department stores. By 2000 we expect that at least 50% of cashiers will use automated equipment. For Scenario S3 we assume that at least 50% of all cashiers will use automated equipment by 1990 and that all checkout stations will be electronic by 2000. Table 3.9 summarizes these assumptions.

TABLE 3.9.   Parameters That Determine Labor Coefficients for Cashiers in 1990 and 2000

Parameters	Scenario S2		Scenario S3	
	1990	2000	1990	2000
Proportion of cashiers not affected by new technology (μ_{23j})	.75	.50	.50	.00
Proportion of cashier time spent in tasks affected by new technology (w_{23j})	1.00	1.00	1.00	1.00
Proportion of time saved by new technology relative to old (γ_{23j})	.10	.10	.15	.15

[a]Inserting these parameters into equation (3-2′) results in proportions in row 8 of Table 3.2.

Other Clerical Workers (IEA #24)

The remaining 50% of clerical workers not discussed above are classified in a variety of clerical occupations that can be divided into two groups based on the potential effects of office automation.

Clerical workers who manipulate data and have little or no interaction with the public will continue to feel a greater impact than any other group of white-collar workers. Although mainframe computers have been able to perform the tasks of back-office clerical workers (such as bookkeepers, file, billing, payroll, and statistical clerks) since the 1960s, computer technology did not affect the multitude of clerical workers in small offices until recently. Small business computers and electronic cash registers that perform a variety of bookkeeping and inventory functions will reduce the need for these workers. As electronic processing becomes more widely distributed, clerical workers in remote locations will also be affected. New microprocessor-based time clocks, for example, calculate overtime hours and vacation days accrued and perform a variety of other data manipulations previously performed by payroll clerks. The latest models of these machines interface with computers that process paychecks, eliminating the need for payroll clerks (Brody, 1983). As another example, office purchasing systems that automate the control of office supplies can reduce the need for stockroom labor. At one company it is alleged that an automated purchasing system permits one person in the stock room to handle the needs of 400 offices in 2–4 hours a week rather than the 60 hours it previously took 1.5 persons (*Administrative Management*, 1981). In short, any function previously performed by clerical workers in this group can be performed faster and more efficiently by auto-

TABLE 3.10.   Parameters That Determine Labor Coefficients for Other Clerical Workers in 1990 and 2000[a]

Parameters	Scenario S2		Scenario S3	
	1990	2000	1990	2000
a. Clerical workers who manipulate data				
Proportion of clerical workers affected by automation ($\mu_{24a,j}$)	.75	.50	.35	.00
Proportion of clerical worker time spent in tasks affected by automation ($w_{24a,j}$)	1.00	1.00	1.00	1.00
Proportion of time saved by new technology relative to old ($\gamma_{24a,j}$)	1.00	1.00	1.00	1.00
b. Clerical workers who interact with public				
Proportion of clerical workers affected by automation ($\mu_{24b,j}$)	.75	.50	.35	.00
Proportion of clerical time spent in tasks affected by automation ($w_{24b,j}$)	.25	.50	.25	.50
Proportion of time saved by new technology relative to old ($\gamma_{24b,j}$)	.50	.50	.50	.50

[a]Taking a weighted average of the two proportions defined by inserting the parameters for *a* and *b* into equation (3-2) results in the proportions in row 9 of Table 3.2. As weights we use clerical workers in *a* and *b* as a share of LAB #24 in 1978 as reported in U.S. Department of Labor (1981).

mated equipment; and the cost of this equipment continues to fall. It is safe to say that these clerical occupations will soon be completely automated. We assume in Scenario S2 that at least 25% of these clerical jobs will be automated by 1990, and 50% by 2000. Under Scenario S3 we assume that the jobs of 65% of these clerical workers could be fully automated by 1990, and by 2000 automation may affect 100% of the clerical workers in this group.

The majority of other clerical workers, however, perform activities that are more difficult to automate since they require interaction with the public; these include bill collectors, counter clerks, dispatchers, interviewers, real estate appraisers, and receptionists. Although most of these jobs will not be eliminated, computer technology will save time in carrying out certain clerical tasks by providing faster access to information.

Under both scenarios, we assume that office systems by 1990 will save 50% of the labor time in 25% of the job tasks of clerical workers who interact with the public. By 2000 we assume that office systems will save time in half these activities. The share of these clerical workers affected by office technology in any year is the same as that for clerical workers who manipulate data. Table 3.10 summarizes these assumptions.

In this chapter we have described our assumptions about the impact of computers on the work of managers, sales workers, and various types of clerical workers in different sectors of the economy, complementing the discussion about factory workers in Chapter 2. Next we turn to education, a large and important service sector which will play a unique role in preparing the future labor force for the changes that will be associated with increasing automation.

REFERENCES

Administrative Management. 1978. The many cases for word processing. Vol. 39 (April): 70–71.

Administrative Management. 1981. Automating the control of office supplies. Vol. 42 (May): 37.

Bikson, Tora K., and Barbara A. Gutek. 1983. Advanced office systems: An empirical look at utilization and satisfaction. N-1970-NSF. Santa Monica, Calif.: The Rand Corporation.

Brand, Horst, and John Duke. 1982. Productivity in banking: computers spur the advance. *Monthly Labor Review* 105 (December): 19–27.

Brody, Herb. 1983. Machines that read move up a grade. *High Technology* 3 (February); 35–41.

Burns, Christopher. 1980. The revolution in the office. In *The Microelectronics Revolution*, ed. Tom Forester, 220–31. Cambridge, Mass.: M.I.T. Press.

Business Week. 1983a. Information technology management. Special Advertising Section, March 21, 88–89.

————. 1983b. How computers remake the managers job. April 25, 68–76.

Byron, Christopher. 1981. Fighting the paper chase: companies look to office automation to boost white collar productivity. *Time*, November 23, 66–67.

Dowing, Hazel. 1980. Word processors and the oppression of Women. In *The Microelectronics Revolution*, ed. Tom Forester, 275–287. Cambridge, Mass.: M.I.T. Press.

EDP Analyzer, "The Experiences of Word Processing," in *The Microelectronic Revolution*, ed. Tom Forester, Cambridge: M.I.T. Press, 1980, pp. 232–243.

Electronics Industries Association. 1982. *1982 Edition Electronic Market Data Book.* Washington, D.C.

Frost and Sullivan. 1980a. *Future Office Systems.* No. A778, 2 vols., New York (June).

————. 1980b. Office automation in the banking industry. No. A839. New York (August).

————. 1982. Business minicomputers for the larger company. No. A982. New York (March).

Gilchrist, Bruce, and Arlanna Shenkin. 1982. The impact of scanners on employment in supermarkets. *Communications of the ACM* (July 25): 441–445.

Gould, John, John Cort, and Todd Horanyecz. 1984. Composing letters with a simulated typewriter. *Communications of the ACM* 26. (April): 295–308.

Green, J. H. 1982. Will more computers mean fewer jobs? *Desktop Computing* (August): 52–54.

High Technology. 1983. Punching in a computer clock. 3 (February): 70.

Hyman, Joan P., and Richard A. Marin. 1983. "Tellerless Branch Gives Staff More Selling Time." *Bank Systems and Equipment.* (February): 40.

Karon, Mary A. 1982. Word processing: When it doesn't work. *Computer World* 16 (March 31): 25, 76.

Maeda, N. 1981. A fact finding study on the impacts of microcomputers on employment. In *Microelectronics Productivity and Employment*, 155–80. Paris, France: OECD.

Marchant, Janet. 1979. Word processing: New perceptions. *Canadian Business* 52 (August): 33–46.

Mortensen, Erik. 1982. Office automation and multifile bibliographic information retrieval. *National Online Meeting Proceedings 1982*, ed. Marthe Williams and Thomas Hogan, 402–3. Medford, N.J.: Learned Information Inc.

Murphree, Mary. 1982. Office rationalization and the changing structure of secretarial tasks: A case study of wall street legal secretaries. City University of New York, Department of Sociology.

Scott, Joan W. 1982. The mechanization of women's work. *Scientific American* 247 (September): 182.

Spinrad, R.J. 1982. Office automation. *Science* 215 (February): 808–12.

U.S. Department of Commerce. 1980a. Bureau of the Census. 1977 census of retail trade, part I vs. summary. 2 vols. Washington, D.C.

————, Bureau of Economic Analysis. 1980b. *New Structures and Equipment by Using Industries, 1972: Detailed Estimates and Methodology.* Washington, D.C.

————. 1982. Fixed reproducible tangible wealth in the United States 1925–1979. Washington, D.C.

U.S. Department of Labor. Bureau of Labor Statistics. 1979. *Technology and Labor in Five Industries.* Bulletin 2033. Washington, D.C.

————. 1981. *The National Industry-Occupation Employment Matrix 1970, 1978 and Projected 1990.* Bulletin 2086. 2 vols. Washington, D.C.

————. Time series data for input-output industries: Output, price and employment. unpublished update on computer tape, DATA, Sic 72, received October 1982.

Uttal, Bro. What's detaining the office of the future. *Fortune*, May 3, 176–196.

Walsh, Willoughby A. 1982. Crying wolf over word processing. *New York Times* (June 3), section D, p. 20.

Technological Change in Education

New information technologies—computers, microprocessors, video recording devices, and inexpensive means of storing and transmitting information—are creating a revolution as important as the invention of printing. Already this revolution is working profound changes in the ways business and industry are conducted. This places new demands on education. . . . Fortunately, the new information technology creates not only new educational needs, but also new and relatively inexpensive ways to meet these needs at home and in school.[1]

The progressive automation of both the production and consumption of goods and services in our economy is placing new demands on our educational system. The increasing use of computers and related devices in office work and manufacturing requires an increasingly technologically literate work force. Certain industries, such as the computer industry itself, are dependent on innovation in fields where knowledge changes rapidly. For this reason, continuing education is required by many professional and technical workers to remain current and productive in their disciplines and in some cases for renewal of their licenses. Virtually all workers will use computer-based information systems in some capacity, and conventional education will increasingly include instruction with and about computers. As the school system develops new curricula, teachers will need additional training. For home use, personal computer manufacturers already provide simple educational packages. This market can be expected to grow considerably in the future to supplement traditional forms of education and to provide formal or informal job training and recreation.

It has traditionally been assumed that education is for the young, work is for early and mid adulthood, and that neither is appropriate in old age. While the location, the hours of instruction, and the structure of educational programs reflect this assumption, increasing numbers of

1. Arthur S. Melmed (1982a).

students and potential students do not fit that pattern. Another attribute of conventional education is its method of instruction, typically a one-way flow of information from teacher to student in a classroom. Two relatively new forms of education based on presently available technologies, computer-based instruction (CBI) and instructional television (ITV), provide electronic courseware, which is well suited to both the lifelong learning concept and the development of new ways of learning.

The purpose of this chapter is to describe quantitatively, as well as qualitatively, how economy-wide technological change may affect education. We examine both conventional education and new technologies and describe ways in which our educational system may be transformed by the use of electronic courseware. The input structures for conventional education and electronic courseware are described in the section entitled, "The Production of Education." The new forms of education will be used by three major groups—industry, conventional education, and households—and the following section, "The Use of Instructional Television and Computer-Based Instruction," describes three alternative scenarios about the use of electronic courseware up to the year 2000.

Our present educational system has been experiencing an increased dropout rate and declining average daily attendance, increased numbers of students performing below grade level, and declining scores on various tests. Seventy-five percent of firms in one survey provided their employees with internal training programs in basic skills which were apparently not learned in school. AT&T, for example, spends $6 million annually to train about 14,000 employees in basic reading and mathematics skills (Center for Public Resources, 1982). Another survey found that 35% of corporations provided some high-school level training for their employees, and the skill levels of those not hired may be even lower.

It has been argued that education is a mature industry and further investment in existing educational technologies will not significantly improve its quality or alleviate its problems. Indeed, our system of education will have to be slowly but fundamentally transformed in order to provide its students with a conceptual framework and skills that make it possible for them to function productively in a changing society.

Conventional educational technology utilizes chalk and blackboard, books, maps, and wall charts; the media are print and speech. Technological change in education has expanded the tools used for learning from mostly written, teacher-mediated and controlled techniques to include the use of video presentation and computers, with the potential for fostering a more active participation by the student. Probably the most notable developments in education today are occurring in interactive technologies, mainly computer-based instruction, where the learner determines the speed and sequence of the program, and video-based instruction which can offer new freedom in scheduling the time and location of classes. While these forms of electronic courseware will affect both the content and the delivery of education, this study concentrates on their impacts on educational delivery.

Computer-based instruction (CBI) requires a computer, access terminals, and either a television or a teleprinter with a keyset. Early systems were based on large computers, either on the premises or through telecommunication links. The smaller, inexpensive, independent microcomputers—which have been actively marketed on the national level only since 1978—already outnumber terminals attached to large computers in educational applications by 3 to 2 (U.S. Department of Education, 1982). Software consists of a computer language for interaction and the courseware itself in the form of prepackaged lessons. First developed in the 1950s to train computer industry personnel, CBI entered schools on an experimental basis in the 1960s. Programmed Logic for Automated Teaching Operations (PLATO) was the first major, and is still the most ambitious, system. It was developed in the 1960s at the University of Illinois with support from Control Data Corporation and the National Science Foundation. A microcomputer version has recently been made available.

Schools still use computers more for records, bookkeeping, and other administrative tasks than for educational purposes. However, in the 18 months between fall 1980 and spring 1982, personal computers intended for educational purposes increased from 31,000 to 96,000 (over 100% annually), while all school computer terminals grew about 14% during the same period (Melmed, 1982b). Computers in schools are expected to reach 980,000 by 1986 (Geller, 1983), growing at an annual rate between 1982 and 1986 of 46%. About 35% of all public schools now make at least one computer terminal or microcomputer available to students, the majority in secondary schools. In 1981–82 $28.5 million was spent on educational software, estimated to grow to $120 million in 1985.

Despite the breakthrough in hardware, results to date in schools using CBI have been mixed. While American programs have typically emphasized the choice and financing of hardware, a recent French experiment indicates the importance of software and teacher training.

Computers were introduced into some French secondary schools in an experimental program from 1970 to 1976 (Hebenstreit, 1980). Over this period, 600 teachers received full-time training, at the end of which each teacher developed a courseware package. An additional 5,000 teachers were trained in applications of computers in the classroom. More than 500 courseware packages were written, and over 7,000 copies of these packages are now in use. The program is considered to be very successful, and its success is attributed to the identification of the crucial role of the teachers. Of the total budget, 70% was devoted to teacher training and release-time; and only 30% was spent on hardware. The underlying assumption of this program was that better quality courseware would be developed by teachers given some computer training than by computer specialists with some help from teachers.

In the U.S. most observers assume that the schools will buy courseware, like textbooks, from private firms (Melmed, 1982b). The small size of the present market, due in part to the high cost and limited quality of available software, dampens the incentive of the private sector to commit additional resources. A major initiative on the part of schools will be required before a large market for software can develop. While most courseware will be purchased, a significant number of schools do create their own. One recent study found that 20% used locally produced software only and 55% used a combination (Harvard University Graduate School of Education, 1982). Two major computer companies, Tandy and IBM, have proposed extensive teacher-training programs.

The use of computers in education has been classified into three categories—tool, tutor, and tutee (Taylor, 1981). The computer as tool functions merely as a powerful calculator. As tutor, CBI can be used in drill and practice, essentially a reproduction on the computer of exercise workbooks presently used in schools. Simulation is a more sophisticated version stressing applications of what has been learned. This mode provides more personal attention for the individual student but is essentially an extension of conventional learning procedures. The computer must be programmed by experts and provided with expensive courseware.

In the tutee mode, students "teach" the computer and in the process they learn about the subject, the computer, and how they themselves think. Students learn to program the computer themselves; they learn concepts, not facts. An example of this mode is the LOGO system developed by Seymour Pappert and his colleagues. The computer as tutee is still viewed as experimental and requires an exceptional teacher but is bound to become increasingly important.

Currently the most extensively used form of CBI is computer-assisted instruction (CAI) which falls under the tutor mode. Schools now consider computer literacy the top priority of CBI, followed by presenting a challenge to high achievers and enriching the learning experience (U.S. Department of Education, 1982). Fewer than half report using CBI for remedial purposes or drill and practice, although drill and practice does dominate in elementary schools, the level with the least computer use (*Instructor*, 1982).

Video-based instruction, mainly instructional television (ITV), is the other major component of electronic courseware. An early example is Sunrise Semester, an ambitious general adult education program which began in the late 1950s and recently ended broadcast due to low station membership. The Appalachian Community Service Network broadcasts more than 64 hours a week with over 1.1 million subscribers, providing both one- and two-way education and teleconferencing services. The University of Idaho Video Outreach Program expects household viewers to reach 41,000 by 1990, about 5% of the state's population (Grayson and Biedenbach, 1982), and the University of Pennsylvania recently announced plans to initiate a similar program. These programs respond to a specific need of industry, professionals, or the local community, define relatively narrow goals, and emphasize the quality of the product. The prime target for educational programs has been graduate level education for scientists, engineers, and managers, as part of formal on-the-job training programs.

Video-based instruction degree programs in the scientific and management disciplines began on a local basis in the late 1960s. Typically, the instructor presents the material to a regular, on-campus class but in a modified classroom which allows simultaneous live broadcast with or without talkback or taping for cassettes. Those viewing the class by television may be tutored by a special assistant on the job, a senior engineer at the firm, or through periodic visits by the instructor.

These programs originated as a response to professional and industry needs by individual universities such as MIT, Stanford, and Colorado State. The universities are now organizing into consortia for individual professions. One such effort is the Association for Media-Based Continuing Education for Engineers (AMCEE) whose 22 member universities have contributed 450 courses on cassettes and account for over 85% of all off-campus ITV in engineering. Of about 1 million working engineers in 1980, 44,000 or 4.4% were enrolled in graduate degree programs via ITV at their places of work (Baldwin and Down, 1981). The majority were under 35 with only a B.S. degree.

The education system is very decentralized, almost a cottage industry, resistant to change on a large scale. In the early days, computerized instruction was often motivated by a desire to increase productivity in education; automating education was supposed to be cost-effective (Baldwin and Down, 1981). At the present time the cost of producing a video cassette of a class is low. But high-quality CBI courseware is expensive to develop and, more importantly, CBI has not yet been successfully integrated into the overall educational curriculum.

As acceptance grows and production technology matures, CBI will come into much wider use; however, it will never completely replace ITV. Video presentation will have an important role whenever talkback participation, dramatization, and demonstrations are required. A demonstration is necessary to teach scientists new experimental techniques and in many aspects of the training of health workers. The American Bar Association found video indispensable for certain kinds of training and established the Consortium for Professional Education in 1975 to teach such things as courtroom techniques and jury selection which require dramatization (Grayson and Biedenbach, 1982). Video presentation is ideally suited to exposing more people to charismatic teachers.

As the industry develops, there will be much greater use of combined video and computer-based learning, particularly video disc technology which combines the student-paced, interactive learning of CBI with the visual presentation of graphics or documentation necessary for many subjects. The visual presentation may also enliven educational packages, making the subject more interesting and tangible to the student and improving both the quality and the range of subjects suitable for CBI.

It will become increasingly difficult for those who have had no exposure to computer technology to function comfortably on the job and even in their social lives. Legislation is before Congress now to provide tax credits for computer purchases to households and schools, and a national policy about computer literacy and public education will need to be formulated.

The Production of Education

Four separate educational sectors have been represented for this study: public and private conventional education (IEA #89, 83) and two sectors producing electronic courseware (IEA #87, 88). The corresponding input structures are described in this section.

Conventional Education

Official input-output (IO) tables treat public and private education differently although they deliver roughly the same output with similar input structures. Private education is a producing sector within the technical matrices and delivers its output to actual users, mainly households. Public education is represented as part of government final demand. This treatment is the outcome of early debates about the appropriate representation of nonmarket activities in the national accounting framework (Gilbert et al., 1948).

We have moved public education inside the matrices as a separate education sector (IEA #89). To accomplish this for the years 1963–1977 required distinguishing capital investment from current account inputs because capital purchases for public education, as part of government final demand, were combined with current account. Capital purchases for past years were estimated based on the purchases of private education (from the CFTs), and the remaining flows were divided by total output (discussed below) and moved into the A matrix. Columns in the other technical matrices were assumed to be the same as for private education. In the new representation, the entire output of the sector is absorbed by households.

The other change from the official data regards the measure of educational output. Education, like other so-called service sectors, has no physical product identifiable as its output, and in the official accounts the value of its output is defined as the sum of its input costs. The official price deflator, in turn, is based on the changing cost of labor inputs. These conventions produce somewhat arbitrary measures of change in real output.

The principal activity of schools is to educate students, and we defined the unit of educational output as a student-year; total enrollment was weighted to reflect the costs of educating students at different levels in terms of equivalent primary-school students. In the future, the BEA will disaggregate education by level in the IO tables so this weighting will not be necessary.

The Department of Education estimates that the annual cost of educating a secondary-school student is 50% higher than for a primary-school student, so the former receives a weight of 1.5. While higher-education costs per student vary considerably, they have been on the average about 2.5 times the cost per primary-school student. We have used this weight with two part-time students considered equivalent to one full-time student. Table 4.1 shows numbers of students enrolled in the U.S. between 1963 and 1980 with projections for 1990 and 2000 and their equivalents in terms of primary school student-years. A change of unit (from dollars' worth to students) was performed for the public and private educational sectors in the technical matrices for 1963–1977. For future years, the totals shown in Table 4.1 were interpreted as projected demand.

For 1963–1977 the input structures for the public and private education sectors used in the IEA model are as given in the official data, adjusted in the ways described above. For future years this structure is maintained with additional purchases of electronic courseware, to be described in the following section, resulting in increased cost per student.

Over the period covered by the historical data, per student real costs have been increasing for labor, intermediate, and capital inputs. While the public sector dominates education, with 88% of total enrollment and expenditures in 1972 of $64 billion compared to $12 billion in the private sector, the trends in cost per student have been similar for public and private education.

There is, however, a persistent gap between the level of public and

TABLE 4.1.   Output of Education (IEA #83, 89), 1963–2000 (Thousands of Students)

Year	Elementary	Secondary	Higher education	Total	Adjusted total[a]	Adjusted total public education[a]	Adjusted total private education[a]
1963	34,504	12,120	4,234	51,908	61,667	49,345	12,322
1967	36,752	13,790	6,401	56,943	70,912	57,503	13,409
1972	34,953	15,377	9,215	59,545	78,506	64,016	14,490
1980	31,619	15,300	11,600	58,519	76,679	64,501	12,178
1985	31,500	13,700	11,350	56,550	75,479	63,263	12,216
1990	35,000	12,100	11,100	58,200	76,030	63,576	12,454
2000	37,200	14,900	11,100[b]	63,200	82,036	69,018	13,018

Sources: Frankel (1981); Frankel and Gerald (1982); Grant and Eiden (1980).

[a]Equivalent in terms of primary school student-years. See explanation in text.

[b]The National Center for Education Statistics does not have an estimate for higher education in 2000, but expects enrollment to increase in the mid 1990s as the 18–25 year-old group increases. The 1990 estimate is a lower limit for 2000.

private costs, the latter usually higher. For all levels the trend has been toward increasing enrollment per public school, especially in higher education, while in private schools the average number of students increased slowly if at all (Grant and Eiden, 1980). The difference in higher-education enrollment also contributes to the cost gap: higher education has accounted for a much greater proportion of total private than public enrollment with only a quarter as many students per school (in 1972).

One factor contributing to the overall increase in costs is the changing product mix. Between 1963 and 1972, the share of secondary-school students remained fairly constant for both public and private schooling but elementary school enrollment declined from 69 to 60% in public education and from 64 to 51% in private education while higher education's share rose from 6 to 13% and from 20 to 30% in public and private schools, respectively.

Labor cost is the single largest input to education, and its share of total expenditures has risen since 1963 in the private sector and declined somewhat in the public sector. The most important intermediate inputs are the same for both public and private education: Business Services, Eating and Drinking Places, Utilities, Transportation, and Maintenance and Repair. The five major manufactured inputs are Printing and Publishing, Paper and Allied Products, Miscellaneous Manufactures (mainly athletic goods, pens, pencils, art supplies, and marking devices), Chemicals and Drugs, and Petroleum and Plastic Products (in which the main entries are cleaning supplies, paints, motor vehicle lubricants, and gas). Real Estate is a large intermediate input.

Electronic Courseware

Some CBI courseware is currently produced by independent firms, including manufacturers of personal computers, and some is by individual users. Much of the existing electronic courseware consists of ITV tapes and broadcasts of regular classes, generally produced in affiliation with institutions of higher education.

Electronic courseware was not combined with the two existing education sectors because the input structures differ and the outputs may be "consumed" independently. Instead the IEA sectoral classification is expanded to include CBI (IEA #87) and ITV (IEA #88), bringing the total number of education sectors to four. Following the literature, we measure CBI output in 1-hour packages and ITV output in 30-hour courses.

The data about ITV presented in this chapter are based on studies which provide a detailed input structure in physical units and costs (Morris, 1974). Courses may be taped or broadcast live and an average of the two was assumed. The SURGE program at Colorado State University provided the taped course input structure and Stanford's Instructional Television, the live broadcast. Table 4.2 shows the technical coefficients for ITV at the present time. This input structure is assumed to remain unchanged through the year 2000. Costs are measured on a per-viewer basis, and ITV output represents the total number of viewers taking a 30-hour course without regard to how many distinct courses are viewed.

TABLE 4.2. Input Coefficients for ITV (IEA #87), 1980 to 2000 (Dollars of Input in 1979 Prices per 30-Hour Course)

Code	Sector	Interindustry coefficients	Capital coefficients
22	Other Furniture and Fixtures	0.1777	3.3515
23	Paper and Allied Products	3.3327	—
25	Printing and Publishing	1.5506	—
51	Office Equipment	0.1454	2.4309
53	Electric Industrial Equipment	0.1858	6.7192
55	Electric Lighting and Wiring	3.3677	
56	Radio and TV Equipment	0.9852	18.7606
57	Electron Tubes	0.1131	2.1805
59	Electronic Components, nec.	0.1454	2.6893
64	Scientific and Controlling Instruments	0.0727	1.4133
65	Optical, Ophthalmic, and Photographic Equipment	0.0242	0.4684
67	Transportation and Warehousing	8.3425	—
68	Communications, except Radio and TV	1.6152	—
77	Business Services	15.5060	—
85	Government Enterprises	1.5506	—

Code	Occupation	Labor coefficients (worker-years per 30-hour course)
17	Managers, Officials, Proprietors	0.0003
16	Other Professional and Technical Workers (TV Technicians and Engineers)	0.0011
19	Stenographers, Typists, Secretaries	0.0007
25–28	Maintenance and Construction Workers	0.0006
52	Laborers	0.0014
14	Teachers	0.0014

CBI output is defined as the total number of 1-hour courses developed, independent of the number of copies or individual users. The school system is the major user of CBI, and it is assumed to make additional copies as required.

A 1-hour CBI package is estimated to cost $30,000 in 1980 dollars for direct technical inputs, mostly the labor of teachers and computer programmers. An additional $90,000 per package is required for overhead, including support services, management, marketing, and profit, which we represent as a purchase from Business Services (IEA #77). Under Scenario S3, which assumes a greatly expanded market, overhead per unit of output can be expected to fall. The rest of the input structure is assumed to remain unchanged. Technical coefficients for CBI are shown in Table 4.3. (Scenario S3′ is described in the section on conventional education below.)

The Use of Instructional Television and Computer-Based Instruction

Industry Use of Electronic Courseware

Certain sectors of the economy have made formal, on-the-job training an integral part of their research and development. We expect to see

TABLE 4.3. Input Coefficients for CBI (IEA #88) Under Scenarios S2, S3, and S3′ in 2000

Code	Sector	Scenario		
		S2	S3	S3′
		(dollars of input in 1979 prices per 1-hour course)		
Interindustry coefficients				
23	Paper and Allied Products	$ 200	$ 200	$ 200
77	Business Services	90,000	30,000	90,000
Capital coefficients				
50	Electronic Computing Equipment	8,000	8,000	8,000
56	Radio, TV, and Communications Equipment	800	800	800
Code	Occupation	(worker-years per 1-hour course)		
Labor coefficients				
6	Computer Programmers	0.5	0.5	0.5
14	Teachers	0.5	0.5	0.5

the greatest future use of electronic courseware in the following sectors:

- Electronic Computing and Related Equipment
- Communications
- Radio, TV, and Communications Equipment
- Aircraft and Parts
- Scientific and Controlling Instruments
- Chemicals (Biogenetics)
- Business Services (Business Management, Computer Programming, and Commercial Research and Development)
- Finance
- Insurance
- Health

Scientists and engineers in industry will pursue "continuing education" both because knowledge is changing rapidly in their specialities and because the number who complete a graduate education is declining—presumably because high starting salaries are offered to those with a B.S. and financial support for graduate study is low. In addition, many professors are leaving the universities for higher-paying jobs in industry, reducing the capacity for producing future scientists and engineers.

Surveys indicate that time is the most serious obstacle to continuing education while working, particularly travel time and the inflexibility of class scheduling (Grayson and Biedenbach, 1982). Electronic courseware offers a solution to these interrelated problems since it can be administered in the work place, alleviating the scheduling constraints and making specialized classes and a small number of outstanding educators available to many people. Assignments can be done with the company's laboratory equipment and computers which are often more up-to-date than those found on campus. Mainly ITV, and very little CBI, has been used in this type of technical training, and our scenarios assume that this trend will continue.

In 1980 4.4% of working engineers participated in degree programs via ITV, taking a minimum of one course per year. We assume that a similar rate (0.04 ITV courses per employee) applies to scientists. This does not include additional courses beyond the minimum degree requirements or any courses viewed in nondegree training programs.

To determine the use of ITV by scientists and engineers in specific sectors, we made use of the percentages of those personnel receiving all types of formal on-the-job training according to a study prepared by Cooke (1982) for the Office of Technology Assessment (OTA). These are shown in Table 4.4. The industry-wide average shown in this table is 18%, about four times that for ITV alone (4.4%); therefore we assume that use of ITV in 1980 is one-quarter of the rates shown in Table 4.4. ITV is expected to experience rapid growth, and the percentages reported in Table 4.4 for 1972–73 for all formal training are assumed under Scenario S2 to hold for ITV alone by the year 2000. Each user of ITV is assumed to take one 30-hour course per year.

Table 4.4 also shows other sectors, not included in the OTA study, which are expected to use ITV for formal training of scientists and engineers in the future; the reported rates are based on similarity to other sectors.

Industrial use of ITV courses in 2000 is quantified for alternative scenarios in Tables 4.5 and 4.6. The numbers reported for Scenario S2 in Table 4.5 are taken directly from Table 4.4 with the exception of Business Services. The subsectors of Business Services identified in Table 4.4 are assumed to account for about half the scientists and engineers employed in the sector as a whole.

TABLE 4.4. Scientists and Engineers Receiving Formal On-the-Job Training in 1972–73 (Percentages)

Industry	
Ordnance and Accessories[a]	31.2%
Chemicals and Selected Chemical Products	22.2
Fabricated Metal Products	15.3
Machinery except Electrical	18.6
Electronic Computers & Office Machinery	46.3
Electrical Machinery	30.1
Electronic Apparatus	28.0
Aircraft and Parts	25.4
Motor Vehicles and Equipment	31.2
Economy-Wide Average	18.0%
Communications[b]	34.8%
Instruments	30.4
Business Services	
Commercial R&D	15.2
Business Management	15.2
Computer Programming	15.2

[a]This group of sectors from Cooke (1982).

[b]Following sectors are IEA estimates.

TABLE 4.5. Use of ITV (IEA #87) by Scientists and Engineers (LAB #1–8) in 2000 (30-Hour Courses per Scientist and Engineer)

Code	Sector	Scenario S2	Additional use under Scenario S3 for selected occupations	
12	Ordnance and Accessories	.312	—	
26	Chemicals and Selected Chemical Products	.222	1.00	Natural Scientists (LAB #5)
			.50	Other Engineers (LAB #4)
39–41	Fabricated Metals	.153	—	
42–49, 52	Machinery	.186	—	
50–51	Computers and Office Machinery	.463	1.00	Electrical Engineers (LAB #1)
53–55, 57–60	Electric Machinery	.301	1.00	Electrical Engineers
56	Radio, TV, and Communications Equipment	.280	1.00	Electrical Engineers
61	Motor Vehicles	.312	—	
62	Aircraft	.254	1.00	Other Engineers
64	Scientific and Controlling Instruments	.304	1.00	Electrical, Industrial, Mechanical Engineers (LAB #1,2,3)
68	Communications (except 69)	.348	1.00	Electrical Engineers
69	Radio and TV Broadcasting	.348	1.00	Electrical Engineers
77	Business Services	.076	1.00	Electrical, Industrial, Mechanical Engineers

TABLE 4.6. Use of ITV by Other Workers in 2000 (30-Hour ITV Courses per Worker)

Code	Sector	Managers (LAB #17)		Other workers	
		S2	S3	S2	S3,S3'
12	Ordnance and Accessories	.045	.090	—	—
26	Chemicals and Selected Chemical Products	.045	.090	—	—
50–51	Computers and Office Machinery	.045	.090	—	—
53–55, 57–60	Electric Machinery	.045	.090	—	—
62	Aircraft	.045	.090	—	—
64	Scientific and Controlling Instruments	.045	.090	—	—
68, 69	Communications	.045	.090	—	—
73, 74	Finance and Insurance	.045	.090	—	—
77	Business Services	.011	.023	.050	.100
	Other Professional Technical Workers (LAB #16)				
81	Hospitals	.011	.023	.125	.250
	Health Professionals (LAB #10–13)				
82	Health Services excluding Hospitals	—	—	.031	.063

Under Scenario S3, employees in the dominant engineering or scientific occupation in a given industry are assumed to receive one unit of ITV in addition to the usage by other scientists and engineers assumed under Scenario S2. For example the usage rate for electronic engineers in the computer industry will be 1.00 and the rate for all other engineers and scientists will be 0.463. These numbers are shown in the last column of Table 4.5.

Electronic courseware has also been used to train managers: the MBA program is currently a major part of ITV offerings and is growing rapidly. Many states have begun to impose educational requirements for license renewal especially for lawyers, accountants, architects, and various health professionals. The American Hospital Video Network, for example, is developing a program to provide continuing education and medical news to all hospitals in the U.S.

Rates of ITV use in 2000 by workers other than scientists and engineers are shown in Table 4.6; in all cases this use is assumed to be twice as intensive under Scenario S3 (and S3') as under Scenario S2. The economy-wide average use of 0.18 courses per worker under Scenario S3 is assumed for high- and middle-level managers who comprise about half the IEA managerial classification for LAB #17, yielding a coefficient of 0.090 for all sectors except Business Services and Hospitals. In these two sectors, managers eligible for ITV-based training comprise one-eighth the IEA classification, yielding a coefficient of 0.023.

Health and various other professionals will provide a large market for ITV products, but these will be slower to develop than the scientist, engineer, and manager markets (Grayson and Biedenbach, 1982). These professionals, especially those in service industries, require specialized training, often for license renewal, rather than standardized degree programs which can be taped from a conventional, college-based class. Health-care institutions are small, decentralized, and independent and tend to arrange their training programs internally.

Lawyers, accountants, and architects were estimated to account for 80% of the occupational category Other Professional and Technical Workers (LAB #16) employed by the Business Services sector. Under Scenario S2 it is assumed that one-quarter of these professionals, or 20% of Other Professional and Technical Workers, obtain additional training; and 25% of these, or 5%, use ITV by 2000. This rate is doubled under Scenario S3.

Hospitals have always provided a disproportionately large amount of training because their extensive, centralized facilities, often affiliated with a medical school, are well equipped for this purpose. Under Scenario S2, 12.5% of all health professionals employed by hospitals, but only 3.1% of those in other health services, use ITV. The latter assumption is based on existing or proposed educational requirements for license renewal for these professionals. Again, these rates are doubled under Scenario S3.

Under all scenarios the use of ITV is assumed to begin in 1980 at one-quarter the rates shown for Scenario S2 in 2000 (for an industry-wide rate of 4.5%) and to increase linearly, reaching the full value in 2000, except for Hospitals and Other Health Services. These two industries begin to use ITV in 1990 under Scenario S2, and in 1985 under Scenario S3 in an amount equal to one-tenth the value shown for Scenario S2 in 2000.

The information given in Tables 4.5 and 4.6 is assembled to produce row #87 of the A matrix for a given year, showing the use of ITV per unit of each sector's output, in the following way. The parameters describing the use of ITV per worker by occupation (i) for each industry (j) in a given year (t), k_{ij}^t, are arranged in a matrix of 53 rows and 89 columns—exactly the form of the L matrix of labor requirements per unit of output, e_{ij}^t. The element-by-element product of these two matrices ($k_{ij}^t e_{ij}^t$) results in a matrix containing ITV requirements per unit of output by occupation and industry. The column sums, which represent total ITV input per unit of sectoral output, become row #87 of the A matrix for that year.

Use of Electronic Courseware by the Public and Private Conventional Education Sectors

ITV in higher education is used essentially for off-campus students and is represented in this study as purchases by industry and households. CBI packages in higher education have been developed by instructors for their own use, and there has been little if any systematic distribution of such courseware at the university level. This section concentrates on the use of electronic courseware at the elementary and secondary level, where ITV will be used for teacher training and CBI for student instruction. The extent of usage will depend upon the availability of computers and prevailing attitudes toward their use in education.

Under Scenario S2 we assume that the use of computers in primary and secondary education grows slowly, reaching 980,000 personal computers by 1990[2] and 1.5 million by 2000: this would provide one

---

2. This number is projected for 1986 by Geller (1983).

terminal for every 30 students by 2000, roughly one hour a week on the computer per student. Under this scenario the computers are used essentially in the tutor mode with purchased courseware and no use of ITV for teacher training. By 2000, only one CBI course per 5000 computers will be developed, and this with no savings relative to present cost structures.

Under Scenario S3, electronic courseware is integrated into primary and secondary school curricula. A plausible national plan outlined by Melmed (1982a) would provide enough hardware to give each student 0.5 hour per day on the computer. With 40 million elementary and secondary school students projected for 1990 and a 5-hour school day, about 4 million computers would be required plus another million for backup, for a total of 5 million. Assuming an average 1982 cost of $1,000 per computer and a 5-year lifetime, Melmed estimates a $1 billion annual cost for hardware, or $25 per student, a very small percentage of total educational costs. Under this scenario computer use continues to grow to about 10 million computers in the schools by 2000. Ten percent of all teachers receive training through ITV by 2000.

Scenario S3' also assumes a rapid growth in this form of education but with the initiative taken mainly by households rather than schools. Nonetheless, there will be twice as many computers in schools as under Scenario S2, for a total of 3 million by 2000. High schools provide the basic skills required in the work place, such as computer literacy and word processing, and also use electronic courseware in mathematics and science classes. The rate of courseware use is the same as under Scenario S2; and while some teacher training is required, ITV is not used for this purpose.

Purchases of CBI and ITV are easily obtained using the parameters summarized in Table 4.7.

Use of Electronic Courseware by Households

At present almost every household in the U.S. has at least one television set. Twenty-eight million residences were wired for cable by early 1982, and the number will reach 58 million by 1990 (Grayson and Biedenbach, 1982). A large and growing number have personal computers as well, but there is relatively little use of electronic courseware by households at this time. The concept of lifelong education is growing in popularity, but it is unclear what share of this market will take the form of electronic courseware used in the home.

TABLE 4.7.   Use of ITV and CBI by the Public and Private Education Sectors under Scenarios S2, S3, and S3′ in 2000

Scenario	ITV per teacher (30-hour course)	Computers per student	CBI courses per computer (1-hour package)
S2	—	1/30	1/500
S3	1/10	1/5	1/750
S3′	—	1/15	1/500

Children and adults, individually or in small group tutorials, could use electronic courseware for an enormous range of purposes including job-training and retraining programs, informal reading and general education, and the popular "continuing education" programs. Education based in the home could grow very rapidly indeed in light of what some consider a failure of traditional education.

For many workers general academic skills may be more important than the specific vocational training on which high schools have traditionally focused. The word processor, for example, is said to be used more effectively by someone with the basic skills to handle and process information than by an excellent rote typist (Center for Public Resources, 1982). The self-paced, individualized instruction made possible by electronic courseware is particularly important for remedial education where learners may be embarrassed and frustrated in conventional learning structures. Control Data Corporation has developed a CBI package for remedial education which has been successfully used by industry.

Under Scenario S2 we assume that the use of ITV in the home, which started in 1980 at a level of 9000 courses, reaches only 200,000 by 2000, involving limited use for job retraining and mainly professional and general education for the highly educated and affluent and, notably, their children. Twice this amount of usage in 2000 is assumed under Scenario S3 (and S3′). In all cases this usage starts from the same low level in 1980 and grows linearly to 2000.

Under all scenarios we assume that the use of CBI by households begins at near zero levels (10 courses in 1980), grows relatively slowly between 1980 and 1990, and then more rapidly in the next decade. The technology of CBI is less familiar and accessible to most people than that of ITV; thus we expect an initially slower growth of usage. Scenario S3′ corresponds to the most intensive household usage, com-

TABLE 4.8.   Use of ITV and CBI by Households Under Scenarios S2 and
S3 in 1990 and 2000

Scenario	ITV in 2000 (30-hour courses)	CBI in 1990 (1-hour packages)	CBI in 2000 (1-hour packages)
S2	200,000	100	1000
S3	400,000	450	4500
S3′	400,000	600	6000

pensating for the slow adoption in primary and secondary schools. The
total use of ITV and CBI is greatest under Scenario S3 since its use in
the schools can be expected to promote professional and recreational
use at home. CBI is not directly linked to computer use by households
(as it is for education) since household computers will also be used for
games, business, financial, and assorted other purposes. The assumptions about the use of electronic courseware by households are summarized in Table 4.8.

This chapter has described the future use of computer-based learning on the job, at home, and in private and public formal education.
Health care is another large service sector in which the government
plays a significant role. The implications of computer-based automation
in the health-care system are discussed in the next chapter.

REFERENCES

Baldwin, Lionel V., and Kenneth S. Down. 1981. *Educational Technology in
    Engineering*. Washington, D.C.: National Academy Press.
Center for Public Resources. 1982. *Basic Skills in the U.S. Work Force*. New
    York: Center for Public Resources (November).
Cooke, William. 1982. "Labor Management Relations in an Era of Program-
    mable Automation." In *Automation and the Workplace: Selected Labor,
    Education, and Training Issues*. Washington, D.C.: U.S. Congress, Office
    of Technology Assessment (August).
Frankel, Martin M. 1981. Projecting a school enrollment turnaround. *American
    Education* 17 (August-September): 34–35.
Frankel, Martin M., and Debra E. Gerald. *Projections of Education Statistics to
    1990–91*. Washington, D.C.: U.S. Department of Education, National
    Center for Education Statistics.
Geller, Irving. 1983. Business outlook: Apples for teachers pay off. *High Tech-
    nology* 3, no. 4 (April):45.
Gilbert, Milton, George Jaszi, Edward F. Dennison, and Charles Schwartz.
    1948. Objectives of national income measurement. *Review of Economics
    and Statistics* 4 (August): 45.

Grant, W. Vance, and Leo J. Eiden. 1980. *Digest of Education Statistics 1980*. U.S. Department of Education, National Center for Education Statistics.

Grayson, Lawrence P., and Jospeh M. Biedenbach. 1982. *Proceedings 1982 College Industry Education Conference*. San Diego: American Society for Engineering Education.

Harvard University Graduate School of Education, Gutman Library. 1982. *Microcomputer Directory: Applications in Educational Settings*, Cambridge, Mass.: Harvard University.

Hebenstreit, Jacques. 1980. 10,000 microcomputers for french secondary schools. *Computer* 13 (July): 17–21.

Instructor. 1982a."Computers? You Bet I'm Interested!" No. 91 (May): 76–77.

Melmed, Arthur S. 1982a. Information technology for U.S. schools. *Phi Delta Kappan*. 63, no. 5 (January).

————. 1982b. Productivity research and technology in education. Washington, D.C.: U.S. Department of Education. (September).

Morris, Albert J., et al. 1974. Final report on cost effectiveness of continuing engineering studies by television. American Society of Engineering Education.

Taylor Robert. 1981. *The Computer in the School: Tutor, Tool, Tutee*, New York: Columbia Teachers College Press.

U.S. Department of Education. 1982. National Center for Education Statistics. Instructional use of computers in public schools. NCES 82–245. Washington, D.C. (September).

CHAPTER 5

Technological Change
in Health Care

The unprecedented growth in recent years of medical care costs, and of hospital costs in particular, has been due largely to the enormous [growth] of resources [often taking] the form of new technologies, such as intensive care and open-heart surgery. . . . The growth of resources, hence of costs, has been made possible by the parallel growth in third party payment. . . . For all practical purposes, there is no end to the amount of resources that can be absorbed by medical care when the economic constraints are removed.[1]

The health-care system is an increasingly important sector in the national economy. It grew from 5.3% of GNP in 1960 to almost 10% in 1981, by which time it directly employed more than 7.5 million people. The provision of health care has undergone considerable change in organization, services provided, and input requirements for delivering these services. Current debates focus on issues of cost and the determination of what constitutes adequate health care.

Through the first half of this century the health-care system was based on the independent practitioner. However, the delivery of health care has now decisively shifted toward hospitals because of the availability of new technologies requiring specialized personnel and equipment accompanied by the growth of third-party financing.

Health insurance originated in the 1930s to protect individuals requiring hospitalization from personal bankruptcy. By 1950, almost half of hospital costs were covered by third-party payments, mostly private insurance, and by the mid 1970s coverage had risen to 90% (U.S. Department of Health and Human Services, 1982). Third-party coverage for total health-care expenditures since 1929 is shown in Table 5.1.

Until recently, health insurance paid fixed premiums and covered hospital care only; even today most insurance is for hospital care. This policy may encourage unnecessary hospitalization even for routine pro-

1. Russell (1979, p. 156).

TABLE 5.1. Third Party Coverage of Health-Care Expenditures, 1929–1980

Year	Health care as percentage of GNP	Percentage covered by direct payment	Percentage covered by third-party payments		
			Total	Private	Public
1929	3.5%	88.4%	11.6%	2.6%	9.0%
1940	4.0	81.3	18.7	2.6	16.1
1950	4.4	65.5	34.5	12.1	22.4
1960	5.3	54.9	45.1	23.3	21.8
1965	6.0	51.7	48.3	26.7	21.6
1970	7.5	39.9	60.1	25.6	34.5
1980	9.4	32.4	67.6	28.0	39.6

Source: U.S. Department of Health and Human Services (1982).

cedures and an excessive number of tests and procedures per patient. In addition it may reduce the incentive for hospitals to contain costs, in turn allowing supplying industries (e.g., the pharmaceutical sector) the opportunity for substantial mark-ups.

Increasing provision of health-care services is also the product of changing social attitudes. Health care has come to be viewed as a right whose access should not be limited to those who can afford it. Coverage for the elderly and the poor was considerably extended through Medicaid and Medicare legislation in 1966.

There is no unambiguous definition of health-care needs. In addition, there is often a lack of consensus on appropriate treatment even within the medical profession, a difficulty intensified by rapid technological change. A recent *Scientific American* article reported that different rates of surgery in various regions of the country were often explained by physicians' preferences—not differences in population, hospitals, or environmental or other factors (Wennberg and Gittelsohn, 1982). Despite tremendous advances in medical knowledge and technology, or possibly because of them, the definition of adequate health care is elusive. So long as coverage is open-ended, demand seems to be unlimited.

The remainder of this chapter is divided into two sections. The first section describes the major components of the health-care industry and their representation in the IEA model for the period 1963–1977. The second section describes two explicit scenarios about developments in health care in the United States through the year 2000.

The Production and Use of Health Care

The IEA model includes two health-care sectors, Hospitals (IEA #81) and Other Health Services (IEA #82). While the most detailed IO tables decompose the latter sector into two—separating Offices of Doctors and Dentists from the rest—they were aggregated for this study due to the limited availability of systematic data on separate capital and labor requirements.

The conventional IO representation accounts for private and public health care differently, including public health care as part of final demand. State and local governments operate about 30% of all general hospitals, and another 5% are run by the federal government, mostly Veterans Administration. While public hospitals provide some services free of charge, their fees for most services are comparable to the market price. In addition, they use inputs and provide outputs similar to those of private hospitals. For these reasons they closely resemble a government enterprise which is usually included inside the IO table as a producing sector. We have included both private and public health care inside the IO table within the two IEA sectors. All health care is assumed to be delivered to households.

The final demand column in the IO tables describing state and local government purchases for health, welfare, and sanitation is predominantly hospital service; the total value of its purchases was added to the deliveries of private hospitals to households. Since the final demand column by convention includes purchases on both current and capital accounts, the detailed information on the input structure for private hospitals both on the capital and the current accounts was used for the combined sector. The small share of hospital services provided by the Federal government has remained in final demand.

The historical data on capital (*B* and *R* matrices) and labor (*L* matrix) requirements for the two health-care sectors were computed in the general way described in Appendix B. Output of the health-care sectors was deflated to 1979 prices using the official BLS deflators: the Consumer Price Index (CPI) for the daily service charge in the case of Hospitals and the CPI for total medical care, eyeglasses and laboratory tests, physicians' and dentists' fees in the case of Other Health Services. In future work it may be possible to measure real output in terms of actual services provided to different categories of patients, drawing in part on the voluminous information available in Public Health Service documents and specialized studies such as those cited among the references for this chapter.

The remainder of this section is divided into three parts describing structural change in different health care settings in the 1960s and 1970s. This serves as background for the scenarios described in the final section of this chapter which examines the prospects for the next 20 years.

Hospitals

During this century hospitals have been providing an increasing amount of health care. While the number of physicians per 100,000 population declined from 176 in the year 1950 to a low of 131 in 1965, rising slowly to 172 by 1978, the number of general hospital beds per 1000 population has risen from 2.9 in 1920 to 5.0 by 1976, and total days of hospital care increased three-fold between 1930 and 1976 (U.S. Department of Commerce, 1975; U.S. Department of Health, Education and Welfare, 1974b, 1976; U.S. Department of Health and Human Services, 1979b, 1981).

Data describing the changing utilization of hospitals[2] between 1963 and 1976 are assembled in Table 5.2. While the number of hospitals has declined slightly, the average number of beds per hospital grew by 39% over this period. Beds per 1000 population has leveled off at about 5, which is the official government target. The number of days of care (which excludes outpatient and emergency-room care) has increased by 8% while the average length of stay has declined by the same amount, and the number of discharges per 1000 population was 14% higher in 1976 than a decade earlier.

The services provided by a hospital during a typical "day of care" have shifted significantly due to changes in medical practice and in demographics. The rate of surgery per 1000 population has increased 42% in the decade of the 1970s, from 78 to 111. The declining birthrate has reduced the relative incidence of childbirth, which used to be the leading cause of hospitalization. (Newborn infants are not included in the number of discharges.) The median age of the population has been steadily increasing, and the growing proportion of older people—especially women—has distinct health-care requirements.

The combination of a shorter average length of stay and a higher rate of surgery has been accompanied by an increased amount of direct care, paper work, and other support services per patient as well as

---

2. This discussion is about general, short-term, acute-care hospitals. Specialty and long-term care hospitals provide mainly psychiatric or tuberculosis care.

TABLE 5.2.   Utilization of Short-Term Hospitals, 1963–1976

	1963	1967	1972	1976	Percentage change 1963– 1976
Total hospitals	6,710	6,685	6,491	6,361	−5%
Total beds	811,876	958,729	1,044,064	1,068,828	32
Beds per 1000 population	4.3	4.9	4.9	5.0	16
Average beds per hospital	121	143	161	168	39
Number of days of care (1000s)	227,136[a]	238,703	243,528	245,110[b]	8
Discharges per 1000 population	na	146.9	158.3	167.7	14[c]
Average length of stay	7.8[a]	8.4	7.7	7.2[b]	−8[d]

Sources: U.S. Department of Health, Education and Welfare (1974b, 1976); U.S. Department of Health and Human Services (1979b, 1981).

[a] In 1965.

[b] In 1979.

[c] 1967–1976.

[d] 1965–1979

intensified use of various types of equipment. Table 5.3 shows the growth in the number of medical services per case between 1951 and 1971.

Comparison of the input structures according to the IO tables for 1963, 1967, and 1977 makes it possible to identify the major areas of change. The proportion of nominal costs accounted for by intermediate inputs has increased, with the value-added portion—which is mostly the wage-bill—falling from 67 to 62% between 1963 and 1972. Over the same period, the quantity of input to produce a given level of output grew by over 40% in real terms (in 1979 prices), since the unit price increase for the output of hospitals is greater than that for virtually all of its inputs (according to the BLS deflators). While food and drugs are major inputs, the largest increases are for services including data processing: hospitals have generally contracted out instead of hiring their own programmers. Other purchases which have grown as a portion of total costs are various plastic products, marking a trend toward the use of disposable items especially in food services. Chemicals and petroleum products which are major inputs for clinical labo-

TABLE 5.3. Number of Medical Services per Case, by
Type of Service and Diagnosis, 1951–1971

	1951	1964	1971
Laboratory tests			
Appendicitis, simple	4.7	7.3	9.3
Appendicitis, perforated	5.3	14.5	31.0
Maternity care	4.8	11.5	13.5
Cancer of the breast	5.9	14.8	27.4
Myocardial infarction	na	37.9	48.5
Pneumonia, hospitalized	na	6.7	18.6
X-rays			
Myocardial infarction	na	1.3	6.3
Pneumonia, hospitalized	na	2.5	3.6
Cancer of the breast, diagnostic	.7	2.0	2.3
Electrocardiograms			
Myocardial infarction	na	5.4	9.0
Inhalation therapy			
Myocardial infarction	na	12.8	37.5
Pneumonia, hospitalized	na	3.8	2.6

Source: Scitovsky and McCall (1976).

ratory tests have grown more important, reflecting the increase in both
the number and utilization of tests. The portion of costs devoted to photographic equipment has also risen, due to increased use of both X-rays
and photocopying equipment.

The health industry, especially hospitals, has been a major source
of employment growth in the 1960s and 1970s particularly for women
and minorities. Table 5.4 indicates an average annual rate of growth of
8.5% between 1960 and 1978 with the most rapid growth (20.4%)
between 1966 and 1970, when federal coverage was provided for the
poor and elderly. Lower growth from 1970 to 1978 (4.7%) suggests
that the surge in demand has leveled off.

The health-care work force includes those directly delivering care,
clerical workers, and service workers. Health care practitioners are
defined to include physicians, optometrists, pharmacists, podiatrists,
veterinarians, and registered nurses; the remainder are often called
allied health workers.

Hospital labor requirements per unit of output (i.e., labor coefficients) for physicians and surgeons and for registered nurses have not
changed much between 1963 and 1977. Other practitioners are not
separately identified in the IEA occupational classification scheme.

TABLE 5.4.   Health-Care Employment, 1960–1978

	All health care	Hospitals	Hospitals as percent of total	Average annual rate of growth since last benchmark year	
				All health care	Hospitals
1960	1,547,600	1,030,000	66.6%	—	—
1966	2,206,500	1,418,500	64.3	6.1%	5.5%
1970	4,630,900	2,960,400	63.9	20.4	20.2
1978	6,698,400	3,900,300	58.2	4.7	3.5

Source: U.S. Department of Labor (1980).

Allied health personnel account for about two-thirds of the industry's work force and grew more rapidly than any other part of the national work force between 1966 and 1978 (Sekscenski, 1981; U.S. Department of Health and Human Services, 1979a). The complexity of their training requirements and of their responsibility has also increased. More than 100 allied health occupations have been distinguished; often a new occupation is created for each new type of medical technology, and many take on work previously done by practitioners. The IEA occupational classification scheme distinguishes Health Technologists (LAB #13), requirements for which have grown significantly between 1963 and 1977; other allied health occupations are dispersed among clerical and service categories.

In the 1960s allied health workers learned their skills through in-hospital training, and almost none were licensed. Due to technological change accompanied by increased areas of responsibility, the need for "middle-level" health practitioners has emerged in areas such as medical record-keeping and clinical laboratories. Numerous specialties require college-level training, and regulation by licensure is also growing.

A nurse practitioner, nurse midwife, or physician's assistant is said to increase the number of visits a physician can attend to by 25–30%— even more in group practice (U.S. Department of Health and Human Services, 1979c; U.S. Department of Health, Education and Welfare, 1974a). At present there are very few such "physician extenders," and rapid growth in their use for hospital care is opposed by physicians.

Because of the extremely high turnover of RNs in hospitals, various approaches have been formulated (e.g., primary nursing and clinical nurse specialists) to increase their training and expand the scope of their responsibility to include some of the work now done by physicians and some by less-skilled LPNs or nurses' aides. In practice, however, it is the role of the LPN that has been expanding (U.S. Department of Health and Human Services, 1979c; U.S. Department Health, Education and Welfare, 1974a).

Health care has traditionally been characterized by a strict division of labor established by physicians' guilds. Many of the factors discussed elsewhere in this section, coupled with a projected oversupply of doctors by 1990, may lead to substantial changes in the organization and responsibilities of health personnel.

Technological change and in particular computer-based automation have affected all aspects of the operation of a hospital. Computers began to be used extensively in hospitals for bookkeeping, billing, inventory control, and patient records following the introduction of Medicare and Medicaid in 1966 which doubled paperwork per patient. It is estimated that today 20–30% of hospital costs are for the handling of this type of information and could be significantly reduced by the increased use of computers (Mahajan, 1979; Paul, 1982).

Hospital laundries and kitchens have become more efficient through the use of larger-scale and more automated equipment, the introduction of computer inventory control and menu planning, and shared laundry and purchasing operations among hospitals. At the same time, the widespread use of disposable items, from paper plates to disposable gowns and medical equipment, has drastically reduced the cleaning, sterilization, and storage activities.

Health professionals have been reluctant to identify specific cost savings from the application of computers to the delivery of health care, but case studies indicate significant benefits especially in the reduction of congestion and the quality of care. Computers have improved speed and accuracy in controlling test equipment in clinical laboratories. In multiphasic screening centers they handle most procedures in a routine physical exam although their role in diagnosis has been limited (Schwartz, 1982).

A great deal of controversy surrounds the use of many of the new technologies for both diagnosis and treatment because of their high costs in the service of very small, specific patient groups and sometimes their unproven efficacy or undesirable side-effects. Now that the infectious diseases have for the most part been brought under control, the major causes of death are heart disease, cancer, and accidents. Prevention through control of diet, smoking, and unsafe work conditions has not been the major focus of modern medical research.

Cobalt radiation therapy is an increasingly common treatment for cancer. Its high cost is due to both the equipment itself and the need to shield staff and surrounding population (Russell, 1979). Of the 430 people per 100,000 population treated for cancer each year, 70% receive cobalt therapy. It is a short-term palliative with very serious side-effects whose benefits are difficult to assess.

Open-heart surgery requires expensive equipment and extensive supporting staff and facilities. In the late 1960s surgeons were concerned about underutilization of the equipment, but its use has grown rapidly since then and is now about 150,000 interventions a year (Russell, 1979). This growth is explained in part by an aging population with increased insurance coverage, in part because the operation is sometimes now performed as a preventive measure.

In 1973 legislation amending Medicare made kidney dialysis for artificial cleansing of the blood costless for the patient. By 1976 about 32,000 patients were being treated at the cost of $684 million, and the number of patients is expected to grow to 60,000 by the mid 1980s (Altman and Blendon, 1979).

Computerized axial tomography (CAT) scanning is a diagnostic procedure using a conventional X-ray source and injection of a contrast material; a computer processes and displays the image in narrow cross-sections. It is considered as accurate as alternative procedures and probably exposes the patient to less risk. The first scanner was installed in the U.S. in 1973; by mid 1976, 317 had been installed with another 335 on order. The average machine at that time cost about $450,000 (Altman and Blendon, 1979). Considerable economies of scale encourage frequent use, perhaps more than warranted, at a price of at least $200 per scan.

Ultrasound technology, used extensively for diagnosis in obstetrics and cardiology, is one of the bright spots among recent technological developments. The computer analyzes sound waves to produce an accurate image of internal structures at low cost and little or no risk to the patient. It is now standard hospital equipment, and new uses are still being discovered.

Positron emission tomography and nuclear magnetic resonance (NMR) are two new imaging techniques that have not yet been marketed. NMR may replace CAT scanners, providing more information and at less risk to the patient. A nuclear magnetic resonator costs between $1 and $1.5 million.

An important structural change in the organization of health-care delivery has been the emergence of the intensive care unit (ICU). In 1962 only 1 hospital in 18 had an ICU. By the mid 1970s over 5% of all hospital beds were in ICUs and every hospital had at least one such unit (Russell, 1979). ICUs group patients in critical condition into coronary, stroke, respiratory, renal, burn, neonatal, pediatric, and poisoning care units where their treatment involves more labor, equipment, and space than could be devoted to them on a regular ward. An ICU often has its own EKG, X-ray and laboratory units, computers, and closed circuit TV. The nursing staff is typically more skilled and three times as numerous (per patient) as on a regular ward.

In what has traditionally been a not-for-profit, decentralized industry, there is a growing trend toward larger, more consolidated, and often specialized hospitals, and a shift to for-profit status (Shonick, 1981). With the increasing importance of expensive, specialized equipment, these organizational changes are intended to reduce duplication and bureacracy and achieve economies of scale at a time when hospital management is under increasing pressure from private health insurers and government legislators to reduce costs.

Offices of Doctors and Dentists

Between 1965 and 1978 the number of doctors per 100,000 population rose from 131 to 172 and the number of dentists increased from 47 to 53 (see Table 5.5). At the same time the proportion of specialists has grown, and group practice has become an increasingly common arrangement.

TABLE 5.5. Doctors and Dentists per Capita, 1965–1978

	Doctors per 100,000 population	Dentists per 100,000 population
1965	131	47
1970	137	47
1972	146	47
1978	172	53

Sources: U.S. Department of Commerce (1968, 1981); U.S. Department of Health, Education and Welfare (1974b); U.S. Department of Health and Human Services (1980, 1982).

Despite the increasing supply of doctors and dentists, Table 5.6 shows that the rate of utilization has not changed much since 1963 when per capita visits numbered 4.8 to the doctor and 1.6 to the dentist. The nature of consultations with physicians, however, has changed with the virtual elimination of the home visit.

Although Offices of Doctors and Dentists are the most labor-intensive of the health-care sectors, the value-added share of nominal costs has declined from 84 to 77% between 1963 and 1972. This is explained in part by the growth of group practices involving the sharing of clerical, nursing, and laboratory personnel and of capital equipment. In addition, there is increasing use of less expensive, nonphysician labor.

The use of dental auxiliaries has increased tremendously from 70 per 100 dentists in 1950 to 122 in 1976 (U.S. Department of Health and Human Services, 1980; U.S. Department of Health, Education and Welfare, 1974a), and all dentists are now trained in "four-hand dentistry" involving at least one auxiliary. Studies have shown that a dentist with no auxiliaries treats about 30% fewer patients than the average dentist with up to three auxiliaries. Unfortunately, both dentists and their auxiliaries are included in a single residual category (Other Medical Professionals, LAB #12) in the IEA occupational classification.

The services—especially medical services—represent a larger share of costs for Offices of Doctors and Dentists than do manufactured goods. There is also large and growing input from personal and repair services, miscellaneous business services, and professional services— more lawyers, accountants, billing agencies, and servicing for a growing

TABLE 5.6   Visits to Doctors and Dentists, 1963–1979

	Total visits (millions)		Visits per capita	
	Doctors	Dentists	Doctors	Dentists
1963	844	294	4.8	1.6
1967	831[a]	260[b]	4.3[a]	1.3[b]
1974	1,025	342	4.9	1.7
1975	1,056	341	5.1	1.6
1979	1,022	366	4.7	1.7

Sources: U.S. Department of Commerce (1968, 1981); U.S. Department of Health, Education and Welfare (1974b).

[a]July 1966–June 1967.

[b]1968.

amount of sophisticated equipment. The most rapidly growing input to this industry is insurance.

Of the manufactured inputs, periodicals and book publishing are the only significant goods not directly related to medical care. Drugs and petroleum products are both important. The use of surgical instruments and supplies, including syringes, bandages, cotton, and all kinds of tools and equipment, has been increasing rapidly, reflecting new techniques and increased reliance on disposables. Many instruments (e.g., scalpels and syringes) are now disposable.

Other Health Services

Other Health Services is a heterogeneous sector. The largest single component is the nursing-home industry[3]; independent medical and dental laboratories, birth control clinics, blood banks, visiting nurse associations, all nonphysician licensed health practitioners, and health maintenance organizations (HMOs) are also included.

The rapid growth in the use of nursing homes is illustrated in Table 5.7. This can be explained by the aging of the population, the tendency of older Americans to live in households separate from their children, and Medicare coverage for nursing homes starting in 1966.

Other components of this sector have also been growing rapidly. The number of HMOs rose from 20 in 1965 and 26 in 1970 to 265, with 10.5 million members, by 1980. Overall costs to members are estimated to be 15–20% lower than for other forms of delivery (*Business Week*, 1982).

As of 1969 independent laboratories were by law allowed to be headed by licensed nonphysicians. In addition, the large array of new diagnostic techniques has been accompanied by increased demand for laboratory services. As a consequence, the number of independent laboratories has grown considerably. In 1975 there were 15,000 clinical laboratories outside of doctors' offices, about half in hospitals and half independent. The latter attained revenues of about $5.5 billion (Altman and Blendon, 1979).

The diversity of this sector, with its changing product mix, obscures a technological interpretation for changes in the cost structure. This is, however, the only one of the three health-care sectors for

---

3. This was for the first time disaggregated as a separate sector in the official 1977 IO tables released by the BEA in late 1984.

TABLE 5.7.   Nursing Homes, 1963–1973

	1963	1967	1971	1973	Percentage change 1963–1973
Number of facilities	16,701	19,141	22,004	21,834	31%
Beds (1000s)	569	837	1,202	1,328	133
Residents (1000s)	491	756	1,076	1,198	144

Source: U.S. Department of Health, Education and Welfare (1974b).

which the value-added share of nominal costs has risen between 1963 and 1972 (from 63 to 68%). The share of services has also been rising consistently, especially personal and repair services, miscellaneous business services, professional services, and other medical services.

The increased share of costs allocated to food and the declining share for surgical supplies in the aggregate sector reflects the growth of full-board, primarily custodial nursing homes. Miscellaneous plastic products, used throughout the sector, grew rapidly. Most dramatic is the increased share of photographic equipment, used both for X-rays and photocopying.

The Future Production of Health Care

The scenarios described in this section assume that we will continue over the next two decades to improve the "quality" of health care in the sense of devoting more resources to satisfying a given final demand. This implicitly assumes no major breakthroughs in prevention techniques.

These scenarios are based in part on the extrapolation of those past trends that can be expected to continue according to the qualitative analysis in the last section of this chapter. The increased use of computers and office equipment and associated changes in employment for administrative operations in the health-care sectors are discussed in Chapter 3. Other changes in input structure after 1977 are summarized in Table 5.8.

Projections of increased use of specific items of capital through 1990, including CAT scanners and nuclear magnetic resonators, were obtained from market research studies (Gruson, 1982; Portugal, 1982)

TABLE 5.8. Input Structure for Hospitals (IEA #81) and Other Medical and Health Services (IEA #82) Under Scenarios S2 and S3[a], 1978–2000 (Annual Real Rate of Increase After 1977, in Percent)

Code	Sector	Hospitals (IEA #81)	Other medical and health services (IEA #82)
Capital coefficients[a]			
60	Miscellaneous Electrical Machinery	1.6%	—
64	Scientific and Controlling Instruments	1.3	1.5%
Interindustry coefficients			
26	Chemicals	3.7	3.5
28	Drugs	5.8	4.3
30	Petroleum and Related Products	8.1	7.7
31	Rubber	8.1	7.2
64	Scientific and Controlling Instruments	4.2	2.2
65	Optical and Photographic Equipment	8.5	7.9
66	Miscellaneous Manufacturers	4.7	2.2
77	Business Services	8.6	8.0
Code	Occupation		
Labor coefficients[b]			
12	Medical Professionals Other than Physicians and Nurses	1.1	—
13	Health Technologists	2.7	5.7

[a]Increased demand for computers and office equipment and associated impacts on employment are described in Chapters 2 and 3.

[b]Under Scenario S2, these annual growth rates are applied to the 1977 coefficients through 1990, and the 1990 matrices are repeated through 2000. Coefficient growth continues at the specified rates through 2000 under Scenario S3.

and are the basis for the increase in capital coefficients shown in the top panel of Table 5.8.

The middle panel of the table shows projected increases in the use of intermediate goods and services. The rates shown are the average annual rates that obtained between 1972 and 1977. The labor coefficients shown in the bottom panel of the table are also assumed to grow at the average annual rate actually experienced between 1972 and 1977. Under Scenario S3, the average annual percentage increases in coefficients shown in Table 5.8 are compounded over the period from 1978 to 2000. Under Scenario S2, this procedure is followed only through 1990 and the coefficients remain unchanged thereafter.

In this and the preceding three chapters we have presented our scenarios about the future use of computers in factories, offices, and in two important components of private and public services, education and health care. Chapter 6 completes the documentation of the technological assumptions by describing our projections about those final deliveries that have not been described elsewhere.

REFERENCES

Altman, Stuart H., and Robert Blendon, eds., 1979. *Medical Technology: The Culprit Behind Health Care Costs*. Washington, D.C.: U.S. Department of Health, Education and Welfare.

Business Week. 1982. Investors are eyeing HMOs. (June 14): 114.

Gruson, Lindsey. 1983. Technicare's CAT scanner woes. *New York Times* (June 19), section 3, p. 4.

Mahajan, Vijay. 1979. Computers in hospitals: An innovation study. *Technology Forecasting and Social Change* 13 (February): 169–186.

Paul, Lois. 1982. Hospital DP facing massive growth. *Computerworld* 16, no. 32 (August 9): 4.

Portugal, Franklin H. 1982. Medical imaging. *High Technology* 2, no. 6 (November/December): 75–82.

Russell, Louise B. 1979. *Technology in Hospitals*. Washington, D.C.: The Brookings Institute.

Schwartz, Morton D., ed. 1982. *Applications of Computers in Medicine*. New York: The Institute of Electrical and Electronics Engineers, Inc.

Scitovsky, A., A. and N. McCall. 1976. *Changes in the Costs of Treatment of Selected Illnesses, 1951–1964–1971*. Washington, D.C.: U.S. Department of Health, Education and Welfare.

Sekscenski, Edward S. 1981. The health services industry: A decade of expansion. *Monthly Labor Review* 104, no. 5 (May): 9–16.

Shonick, William. 1981. Expanding contracting: Private management of public hospitals in California. *Health PAC Bulletin* 13, no. 1 (November/December): 7–10, 22–32.

U.S. Department of Commerce. Bureau of the Census. *Statistical Abstract of the United States 1968*. Washington, D.C. (1968).

————. *Historical Statistics of the United States, Colonial Times to 1970*. Washington, D.C. (1975).

————. *Statistical Abstract of the United States 1981*. Washington, D.C. (1981).

U.S. Department of Health, Education and Welfare. Public Health Service. *The Effects of Task Delegation on the Requirements for Selected Health Manpower Categories in 1980, 1985 and 1990*. Washington, D.C. (1974a).

————. *Health Resource Statistics, 1972*. Washington, D.C. (1974b).

————. *Utilization of Short-Stay Hospitals, 1974*, Washington, D.C. (1976).

U.S. Department of Health and Human Services. Public Health Service. *A Report on Allied Health Personnel*, Washington, D.C. (1979a).

————. *Utilization of Short-Stay Hospitals, 1977*. Washington, D.C. (1979b).

————. *The Impact of the Health System Changes on the Nation's Requirements for Registered Nurses.* Washington, D.C.. (1979c).

————. *Health Resource Statistics, 1978–79.* Washington, D.C. (1980).

————. *Utilization of Short-Stay Hospitals, 1979.* Washington, D.C. (1981).

————. *Health, U.S. 1981.* Washington, D.C. (1982).

U.S. Department of Labor. Bureau of Labor Statistics. *National Industry by Occupation Employment Matrix 1970, 1978 and Projected 1990.* Bulletin 2086. Washington, D.C. (1980).

Wennberg, John, and Alan Gittelsohn. 1982. Variations in medical care among small areas. *Scientific American* (April): 120–134.

CHAPTER 6

Projections of
Final Deliveries

Deliveries of goods and services to households, many types of government activities, and foreign trade have not been described in Chapters 2 through 5. The IEA model is not yet "closed" with respect to these activities and therefore needs to be provided (from outside sources) with projections of the levels as well as the composition of the goods and services they will require. Projected deliveries for investment purposes, on the other hand, are determined within the dynamic model.

For the present study we did not attempt to make original projections of these final deliveries. Instead we relied on the medium-growth version of the most recent BLS projections which were available at the time this work was being carried out. These projections take the form of a matrix with 156 sectors and 13 categories of final demand for each of two benchmark years, 1985 and 1990, in 1972 prices. Labor employed directly by households and government is not included. A discussion of the BLS methodology can be found in *Monthly Labor Review* (1981) and U.S. Department of Labor (1982).

The BLS final demand matrix was aggregated to a single column of noninvestment final demand, inflated to 1979 prices, and aggregated from 156 to 89 producing sectors for each benchmark year. The resulting final demand vector was interpolated linearly for years between 1977[1] and 1985 and between 1985 and 1990. Sector-specific growth rates for the five-year period between 1985 and 1990 were repeated for the periods 1990–1995 and 1995–2000, and annual final demand was interpolated linearly for the years in between.

In addition to modifications of final demand for education and health, which are described in Chapters 4 and 5, some changes were made to reflect growing use of computers by households and the mili-

---

1. The preparation of the 1977 final demand vector is included in the work described in Appendix B.

TABLE 6.1.   Household Demand for Computers (IEA #50), Versions 1 and 2, 1980–2000 (Millions of Dollars, 1979 Prices)

	BLS Projections	IEA Version 1	IEA Version 2
1980	$169	$ 494	$ 988
1985	219	1,085	2,170
1990	341	2,424	4,848
2000	584	3,494	6,988

tary. Two versions of final demand, differing in the presumed future use of computers in homes and by the government, were prepared in addition to the BLS projections.

At the present time it seems clear that the BLS projections of household use of computers are unrealistically low. Considerably higher projections were prepared by the market research organization LINK (reported in U.S. Congress, 1982). The first IEA version of final demand used the LINK projections for household computer use until 1986, with the average annual growth rate between 1982 and 1986 extrapolated to 1990. Between 1990 and 2000 we assumed that growth would continue at only half this rate. In the second version of the final demand projections, purchases of computers by households in 1985, 1990, and 2000 are double the low estimates. These assumptions are shown in Table 6.1.

In the first version of the IEA projections, the military use of computers is represented by the BLS estimate. The second version is based

TABLE 6.2.   Military Demand for Computers (IEA #50) and Related Services (Part of IEA #77), Versions 1 and 2, 1980–2000 (Millions of Dollars, 1979 Prices)

	Computer hardware		Software and services	
	BLS projections and IEA version 1	IEA version 2	BLS projections and IEA version 1	IEA version 2
1980	366	2,776	590	3,089
1985	377	3,785	819	6,336
1990	670	5,541	1,764	11,810
2000	1,749	11,874	4,603	25,311

on estimates of the future use of computers, software, and related services given by Electronics Industries Association (1980). Half of the software and related services used by the military are purchased from the private sector, shown in our model as an input from Business Services (IEA #77). The use of computers and services in 2000 is extrapolated from 1990 based on the growth rate between 1985 and 1990 anticipated in this source. While these estimates of the military use of computers, shown in Table 6.2, are significantly higher than those prepared by BLS, they are low compared to the present administration's projected military budgets. This policy may, however, be reversed before 2000.

The results reported in Chapter 1 are all obtained using the second version of these final demand projections.

REFERENCES

Electronics Industries Association. 1980. *Department of Defense Digital Data Processing Study: A Ten-Year Forecast*. Washington, D.C.

Monthly Labor Review 104, no. 8, August 1981.

U.S. Congress. Office of Technology Assessment. *Informational Technology and its Impact on American Education*. Washington, D.C. (November 1982).

U.S. Department of Labor. Bureau of Labor Statistics. *Economic Growth Model System Used for Projections to 1990*. Bulletin 2112. Washington, D.C. (April 1982).

APPENDIX A

The Dynamic
Input-Output Model

Probably the most familiar aspect of input-output (IO) analysis is the IO table published for the U.S. economy about every five years by the Department of Commerce and at various intervals by its counterparts in many other countries. This is a rectangular table which, using double-entry bookkeeping, tracks all the transactions that have taken place within the economy in a given year. For this purpose, all private establishments are classified into a specified number of industries, each of which sells its output as inputs to the others. Each industry's output is also sold for various types of final, as opposed to intermediate, use: the destinations of these so-called final deliveries are conventionally designated as households, government agencies, private investment, and (net) exports. Finally, each industry's unit price must cover the costs of additional inputs, mainly labor, profits, and the use of capital, which comprise its value-added.

The format of an IO table is shown schematically in Figure A.1. The actual numbers appearing as consecutive entries in the column marked by x's represent the dollar values of the purchases of a particular industry, say the computer industry, from each industry—including itself—and its value-added. The corresponding row (the 50th row if the computer industry is represented by the 50th column) shows the sales of computers to each industry—including itself—and to final users.

The IO table is turned from a static description into an analytic tool by transforming the flow table described above into a coefficient matrix. Each entry in a given column of the flow table is divided by the total output of the column industry, and the resulting ratio of input per unit of output is called a technical coefficient. The significance of a matrix of technical coefficients is that each column represents an average technology or "cooking recipe" for the production of a single unit of the corresponding industry's output; in fact, the columns of the coefficient matrix can be assembled directly from engineering data without

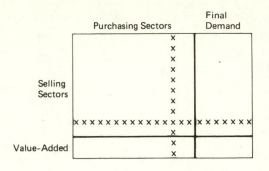

FIG. A.1.   Format of an Input-Output Table.

passing by the flow table and can be measured in physical, not necessarily value, units. This is precisely how the matrices for 1990 and 2000 have been projected for this study.

For analytic purposes, the square industry by industry, or interindustry, portion of the coefficient matrix is designated as the A matrix; it contains the current account requirements (as distinguished from capital requirements) of each sector. The fundamental IO balance equation is written in matrix form as

$$x = Ax + y$$

where x is the vector of total output and y is the vector of final deliveries. This equation means that output is divided into two parts: deliveries to all industries to satisfy their production requirements (Ax) and deliveries to final users (y). The equation can be rewritten as

$$y = (I - A)^{-1}x$$

where I is the identity matrix. $(I - A)^{-1}$ has been called the Leontief inverse matrix; its significance is that it directly relates final deliveries to the outputs necessary to produce them. This simple formulation makes possible numerous experiments. For example, one can

- fix y and determine x for a given A,
- fix x and determine y for a given A,
- change elements of A and repeat above.

Typically it is final deliveries that are specified and outputs that are determined by the computation.

One can in addition assemble information for a matrix of each industry's labor requirements, by occupation, per unit of output (L

matrix) and of each sector's capital stock requirements, by type of capital, per unit of output (K matrix). Then for a given y one can compute not only x but also

$$e = Lx$$

and

$$k = Kx$$

where e is the vector of labor requirements, by occupation, for the economy as a whole and k is the corresponding vector of capital stock requirements.

In the event of technological change when, for example, plastics are substituted for metals in various applications, one can change the corresponding coefficients in the A matrix and make a new computation. In the case in which robots replace welders, one would change coefficients in the K and L matrices. But here a problem arises: when capital requirements change, investment patterns will generally also change. While in the above formulation, or model, investment is specified as part of final deliveries, the level and composition of investment goods are in fact generally determined by technological considerations and sectoral growth.

Investment is the focus of attention in moving from the static to the dynamic IO model. The simplest formulation of the dynamic IO model can be written as follows:

$$x_t = A_t x_t + R_t x_t + B_{t+1} (x_{t+1} - x_t) + y_t$$

Two new matrices have been introduced: R is the matrix of capital replacement requirements per unit of output and B is the matrix of capital requirements for expansion of each sector's capacity. The model now requires a subscript referring to a particular time period, t, because the investment goods purchased by (and produced for) a sector in time t will typically enable it to effectively increase its capacity only at some future time—$t + 1$ in this simple formulation. In this equation final deliveries, y, explicitly exclude investment which is instead completely determined within the model.

Our objective was to design a dynamic input-output model to study the effects on labor requirements in the United States of alternative scenarios of technological change between 1963 and 2000. The starting point was the model introduced by Leontief (1970):

$$x(t) - A(t)x(t) - B(t + 1)[x(t + 1) - x(t)] = y(t) \qquad \text{(A-1)}$$

where x is the vector of outputs, A is the matrix of input requirements on current account, B is the matrix of capital requirements, and y is the vector of noninvestment final demand.[1] Once a model of the type represented by equation (A-1) is solved for the vector of outputs for period t, $x(t)$, the vector of employment requirements by occupation is easily obtained.

In the present formulation, the investment term $B[x(t + 1) - x(t)]$ in equation (A-1) is replaced by expressions formulated in accordance with the following considerations:

Once capacity is in place, it need not be fully utilized and is not reversible.

In each time period, expansion decisions are made for each sector based on recent past growth rates, and capital goods are ordered.

Some capital goods must be delivered several periods before the new facility of which they are part can effectively add to the investing sector's capacity.

Replacement investment is explicitly represented, separately from expansion.

A history of the dynamic input-output model which describes the motivation for the present formulation and a more detailed description of the new model can be found in Duchin and Szyld (1984).

We introduce two additional (vector) variables:

$c(t)$ output capacity during period t

$o(t)$ increase in productive capacity between periods $t-1$ and t

and we define $c(t) = c(t - 1) + o(t)$. If for sector i, $c_i(t) > x_i(t)$, capacity is under-utilized; if $c_i(t) < x_i(t)$, it is over-utilized.[2]

A sector's future capacity requirements are projected several periods in advance, independent of the capacity in place. For that reason we also introduce the vector $c^*(t)$ of projected capacity require-

---

1. In this section of the chapter, time is represented by the letter t in parentheses rather than as a subscript. We reserve the use of subscripts to denote the specific components (e.g., sectors) of a vector.

2. Over- and under-utilization are relative to a presumed state of exactly full capacity utilization. Base-year rates of capacity utilization are specified in the initial conditions (given in Appendix B), and the concept in the model follows whatever interpretation is used in their derivation.

ments for (future) period t and define the increase in capacity in sector i as:

$$o_i(t) = \max [0, c_i^o(t) - c_i(t - 1)]$$

Thus if $c_i(t - 1) \geqslant c_i^o(t)$, then $o_i(t) = 0$, no new output capacity is needed, and $c_i(t) = c_i(t - 1)$. Otherwise, the change in capacity, o, is the increase needed to achieve the projected capacity requirement, c^o.

The investment term in period t could now be written as $B(t + 1)o(t + 1)$, implying that investment goods required to increase the capacity in period $t + 1$ are produced and delivered one period earlier. In fact, we recognize that different types of capital goods may have to be delivered two or more periods earlier. We denote by τ_{ij} the lag between the period when a capital item is produced (by sector i) and the period in which it effectively adds to the capacity of sector j, and by τ_j the maximum lag for any capital good required by sector j (i.e., $\tau_j = \max_i \tau_{ij}$).

Planned capacity expansion in sector j will require τ_j periods for its realization and thus will need to be formulated at least τ_j periods in advance. For the present study we make the provisional, simplifying assumptions that τ_{ij} and τ_j are the same for all capital-using sectors j. Following Johansen (1978, p. 515), we denote as τ_i the lag for capital goods produced by sector i and $\tau = \max_i \tau_i$.

The investment term now becomes

$$\sum_{\theta=1}^{\tau} B^\theta(t)o(t + \theta)$$

where the ij^{th} entry of $B^\theta(t)$, $b_{ij}^\theta(t)$, is the amount of capital produced in period t by sector i to increase the capacity of sector j by one unit in period $t + \theta$.[3] Of course, $b_{ij}^\theta(t) = 0$ for $\theta > \tau_i$.

In the present formulation future capacity requirements, $c^o(t + \tau)$ planned τ periods in advance, are assumed to be determined by recent past changes in sectoral output. In order to prevent excessive expansion plans in time of rapid growth, likely to be followed by a long period of under-utilization, a sector-specific maximum admissible annual rate of expansion of capacity, δ, is imposed. (Only the sector's expansion investment and not its output is potentially constrained by δ. Values for δ are given in Appendix B.) This results in the following expression:

---

3. These capital coefficient matrices $B^\theta(t)$ are related to $B(t + 1)$ of equation (A-1) by

$$B(t + 1) = \sum_{\theta=1}^{\tau} B^\theta(t + \theta - 1)$$

$$c_i^o(t + \tau) = \max \left[1 + \delta_i, \frac{x_i(t - 1) + x_i(t - 2)}{x_i(t - 2) + x_i(t - 3)} \right]^{\tau+1} x_i(t - 1) \quad \text{(A-2)}$$

We can now write the whole model and solve for $x(t)$ for each period from t_0 through the final period t_T. The initial conditions must specify values for

$$c(t_0)$$
$$x(t), \; t = t_0 - 3, \ldots, t_0 - 1$$

Given these initial conditions, we compute c^o, o, and c, in that order, for periods $t_0 + 1$ through $t_0 + \tau - 1$. For each period in turn ($t = t_0, \ldots, t_T$) we first solve for $c^o(t + \tau)$ using equation (A-2). Then we compute the future additions to capacity

$$o(t + \tau) = \max [0, c^o(t + \tau) - c(t + \tau - 1)] \quad \text{(A-3)}$$

and we update the capacity,

$$c(t + \tau) = c(t + \tau - 1) + o(t + \tau) \quad \text{(A-4)}$$

Replacement investment is represented as

$$R(t)x(t)$$

where the ij^{th} entry of the replacement matrix $R(t)$ is the amount of capital goods produced by sector i that must be replaced in order to produce a unit of output of sector j during period t. We can now solve for $x(t)$ from

$$[I - A(t) - R(t)]x(t) = \sum_{\theta = 1}^{\tau} B^\theta(t)o(t + \theta) + y(t) \quad \text{(A-5)}$$

Thus equation (A-1) has been replaced by equations (A-2) through (A-5).

Finally, labor requirements by occupation during period t are obtained as

$$e(t) = L(t)x(t) \quad \text{(A-6)}$$

where the qj^{th} element of $L(t)$ is the amount of labor of occupation q required to produce a unit of output of sector j during period t.

REFERENCES

Duchin, Faye, and Daniel B. Szyld. 1984. A dynamic input-output model with assured positive output (submitted for publication).

Johansen, Leif. 1978. On the theory of dynamic input-output models with different time profiles of capital construction and finite life-time of capital equipment. *Journal of Economic Theory* 19: 513–241.

Leontief, Wassily. 1977. Dynamic inverse. In *Essays in Economics*, 50–70. New York: M. E. Sharpe, Inc.

APPENDIX B

The Historical
Database, 1963—1980

The dynamic model which is described in Appendix A requires extensive data on production, capital, and employment by industry. Most of these data are made available in various publications by the Department of Commerce or the Department of Labor.

The basic sources of information are the IO studies published for 1963, 1967, and 1972 by the BEA, in the Department of Commerce (U.S. Department of Commerce, 1969, 1974a, 1979). The IO table for each of these three years describes the flows of commodities produced and consumed by each industry and the commodities absorbed by different final uses: private consumption, capital formation, government purchases, and foreign trade. The BEA has also produced capital flow tables (CFTs) for 1963, 1967, and 1972 (U.S. Department of Commerce, 1971b, 1975a, 1980), which disaggregate the investment portion of final demand in the corresponding IO table and show the flows of the different fixed capital goods to the industries which use them. The official IO study prepared for 1977 by the BEA was not published until May 1984, but the BLS in the U.S. Department of Labor made available a preliminary IO table for 1977 (U.S. Department of Labor, 1982b).

Price indexes for IO industries and several series on sectoral capital stocks and flows are produced by the BLS which has also prepared detailed occupation-by-industry matrices for 1960, 1970, and 1978. Other sources of information which have been used are described in the course of the discussion.

The preparation of the data required reconciling different classifications and conventions among data sources and from one IO study to the next. Some of the changes correspond to an improvement in methodology. Others are explained by actual changes in the economy; technical change, for example, involves the appearance and disappearance of certain commodities and the industries which produce them. When it was possible, we transformed the earliest data to conform with the latest conventions. Differences and incompatibilities among data sources are explained mainly by the decentralized approach to the collection of government data.

The IEA model is computed on an annual basis and is used to analyze the effects of technological change in the long-term. Linear extrapolation was used to produce matrices of coefficients for the years between the benchmark years for which full detail is available.

The changes required to make conventions and valuation uniform in the different IO studies are explained in this appendix, including a description of the industrial classification used in the model, the treatment of imports, secondary products, and eating and drinking places, and deflation of the data so that all magnitudes would be expressed in 1979 prices.

The following section is devoted to computations required to obtain the three matrices of coefficients A, B, and R. Then data for initial conditions and control totals are described, followed by an explanation of the data on employment by industry and occupation. The description of coefficient matrices for 1978–1980 completes this appendix.

Conventions and Valuation

Sectoral Classification Scheme

One of the first steps in preparing the database involved selecting sectoral and occupational classification schemes and reconciling the existing official data series into these categories. This section describes the sectoral classification scheme used in preparing the A, B, R, and L matrices with particular reference to the BEA IO and capital-flow tables used in their preparation.

The capital-flow tables which enter into the computation of B and R matrices contain columns showing the detailed commodity composition of gross investment in fixed capital for 77 sectors.

The 1963 and 1967 BEA IO tables consist of 368 sectors, while the 1972 BEA IO table and the 1977 BLS IO tables have been further disaggregated to 496 sectors. Several BEA sector codes do not appear at all in our classification. These include so-called Special Industries (Government Industry, Household Industry, Rest of the World Industry, and Inventory Valuation Adjustment) which contain only the value added portion of the corresponding final demand sectors. The "dummy" industries reflect the secondary production of certain goods and vanish when the industry-by-industry table of transactions is calculated. Non-competitive imports (discussed below) are treated as external to the transaction table and are included in value added.

The industrial classification of the BEA IO tables is based on the Standard Industry Classification (SIC). The SIC was revised over the period from 1963 to 1972 [changes are described in the SIC manuals of 1957, 1967, and 1972 (U.S. Executive Office of the President, 1957, 1967, 1972)]. While the changes between the 1957 and 1967 editions were minimal, substantial changes took place between 1967 and 1972. Most sectors at the level of detail of the IEA classification were unaffected, however, and among those that were affected, we were able to ascertain that the impact was small by comparing BLS sectoral outputs conforming to one SIC classification with BEA sectoral outputs conforming to the other. However, the discrepancies were significant for three sectors (IEA #4, Agricultural, Forestry, and Fishery Services; IEA #32, Leather Tanning and Finishing; and IEA #79, Automobile Repair Services). In the absence of further information, the BEA representation for each benchmark year was maintained.

A major objective in determining the sector scheme was to segregate those sectors likely to be major actors in the production or adoption of automated equipment, such as computers and semiconductors. A detailed representation of the important "service" sectors was desirable because of their large employment and intensive use of computers.

The sectoral classification scheme for the IEA database contains 89 sectors, including three newly emerging ones not yet included in official data series; the classification scheme is shown in Table B.1. It follows the 2-digit BEA classification with the following exceptions. The BEA sectors for new and maintenance construction were aggregated into a single construction sector; and federal, state, and local government enterprises were likewise combined into one IEA sector. On the other hand, BEA #51 (Office, Computing, and Accounting Machines) was split into two sectors with computers separated from other office equipment. BEA #57, Electronic Components and Accessories, was split into the rapidly growing Semiconductors and Related Devices, Electron Tubes, and the remainder. Trade was divided into wholesale and retail, and Finance and Insurance are shown separately. BEA #77 was subdivided into Hospitals, Other Health Services, Educational Services, and Nonprofit Organizations. In our scheme, purchases of residential real estate are taken out of the capital matrices and put into final demand because the demand for this investment is not directly deter-

TABLE B.1.   IEA Sectoral Classification and Corresponding BEA Codes

IEA code	Description of sector	BEA code
1	Livestock and Livestock Products	1
2	Other Agricultural Products	2
3	Forestry and Fishery Products	3
4	Agricultural, Forestry, and Fishery Services	4
5	Iron and Ferroalloy Ores Mining	5
6	Nonferrous Metal Ores Mining	6
7	Coal Mining	7
8	Crude Petroleum and Natural Gas	8
9	Stone and Clay Mining and Quarrying	9
10	Chemical and Fertilizer Mineral Mining	10
11	Construction	11, 12
12	Ordnance and Accessories	13
13	Food and Kindred Products	14
14	Tobacco Manufactures	15
15	Broad and Narrow Fabrics, Yarn, and Thread Mills	16
16	Miscellaneous Textile Goods and Floor Coverings	17
17	Apparel	18
18	Miscellaneous Fabricated Textile Products	19
19	Lumber and Wood Products, except Containers	20
20	Wood Containers	21
21	Household Furniture	22
22	Other Furniture and Fixtures	23
23	Paper and Allied Products, except Containers	24
24	Paperboard Containers and Boxes	25
25	Printing and Publishing	26
26	Chemicals and Selected Chemical Products	27
27	Plastics and Synthetic Materials	28
28	Drugs, Cleaning, and Toilet Preparations	29
29	Paints and Allied Products	30
30	Petroleum Refining and Allied Industries	31
31	Rubber and Miscellaneous Plastic Products	32
32	Leather Tanning and Finishing	33
33	Footwear and Other Leather Products	34
34	Glass and Glass Products	35
35	Stone and Clay Products	36
36	Primary Iron and Steel Manufacturing	37
37	Primary Nonferrous Metals Manufacturing	38
38	Metal Containers	39
39	Heating, Plumbing, and Structural Metal Products	40
40	Screw Machine Products and Stampings	41
41	Other Fabricated Metal Products	42
42	Engines and Turbines	43
43	Farm and Garden Machinery	44
44	Construction and Mining Machinery	45

TABLE B.1 *(cont'd)*.   IEA Sectoral Classification and Corresponding BEA Codes

IEA code	Description of sector	BEA code
45	Materials Handling Machinery and Equipment	46
46	Metalworking Machinery and Equipment	47
47	Special Industry Machinery and Equipment	48
48	General Industrial Machinery and Equipment	49
49	Miscellaneous Machinery, Except Electrical	50
50	Electronic Computing and Related Equipment	51.01
51	Office Equipment, Except IEA #50	51 except 51.01
52	Service Industry Machines	52
53	Electric Industrial Equipment and Apparatus	53
54	Household Appliances	54
55	Electric Lighting and Wiring Equipment	55
56	Radio, TV, and Communications Equipment	56
57	Electron Tubes	57.01
58	Semiconductors and Related Devices	57.02
59	Electronic Components, nec.	57.03
60	Miscellaneous Electrical Machinery and Supplies	58
61	Motor Vehicles and Equipment	59
62	Aircraft and Parts	60
63	Other Transportation Equipment	61
64	Scientific and Controlling Instruments	62
65	Optical, Ophthalmical, and Photographic Equipment	63
66	Miscellaneous Manufacturing	64
67	Transportation and Warehousing	65
68	Communications, Except Radio and TV	66
69	Radio and TV Broadcasting	67
70	Electric, Gas, Water, and Sanitary Services	68
71	Wholesale Trade	69.01
72	Retail Trade	69.02
73	Finance	70.01–.03
74	Insurance	70.04, .05
75	Real Estate and Rental	71
76	Hotels, Personal, and Repair Services exc. Auto	72
77	Business Services	73
78	Eating and Drinking Places	74
79	Automobile Repair Services	75
80	Amusements	76
81	Hospitals	77.02
82	Health Services, excluding Hospitals	77.01, .03
83	Educational Services	77.04
84	Nonprofit Organizations	77.05–.09
85	Government Enterprises	78, 79
86	Robotics Manufacturing	—
87	Instructional TV	—
88	Computer-Based Instruction	—
89	Public Education	(final demand column)

mined by the productive requirements of the economy. Public Education and Health are treated as producing sectors which sell to final demand.

Imports

The U.S. IO tables make a distinction between imports which are comparable with domestic production and those which do not have any equivalent produced inside the U.S. The first are called comparable imports. The second are called noncomparable or noncompetitive imports.

The treatment of noncomparable imports does not present any particular problem as it is identical in the four IO studies (1963, 1967, 1972, and 1977) in which noncomparable imports appear as a row.

The treatment of comparable imports changed between the earlier IO studies (1963–1967) and the later ones (1972–1977). In the present work we have adopted the conventions used for the 1972 study and modified the 1963 and 1967 tables to match these conventions. After showing the differences in the two treatments of imports, we describe the procedure used to modify the transactions tables, the final demand tables, and the capital flow tables for 1963 and 1967.

In the 1972 and 1977 IO tables, the total output of each industry measures domestic production and excludes imports. Consistent with this approach, imports are shown as negative entries in a final demand column. Since their valuation must be comparable with the producers' prices used for the domestic production of the same commodity, comparable imports are measured at domestic port value, which includes the external, usually transoceanic, margin required to bring the commodity to the U.S. border and duty owed on this import (see Table B.2). When the transoceanic transportation is provided by a U.S. carrier, the margin is also shown as a positive, offsetting entry in the cell of the import column related to the transportation industry. Duties are also shown as an offset, assumed to be provided by the wholesale trade sector.

For the 1963 and 1967 studies the BEA used a "transfer" treatment of comparable imports for industrial use. As with the case of secondary products, imports were transferred to the industry whose output was comparable. Therefore, there is an additional row for imports, besides the one for noncomparable imports, called "transferred imports." The total output shown for an industry equals its domestic output plus the amount of imports of a comparable commodity. Trans-

TABLE B.2.   Cost Structure of Imports

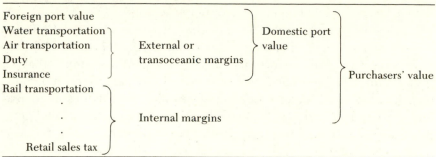

Source: U.S. Department of Commerce (1980, p. 22).

ferred imports are shown at the foreign port value and external margins associated with their shipment are included in the Trade, Transportation, and Insurance rows.

Replicating the 1972 treatment of comparable imports for industrial use in the 1963 and 1967 tables requires three steps:

- The domestic port value of transferred imports is determined by adding the external margins related to these shipments to the foreign port value of the imports shown in the table.
- These values are included as negative entries in a new import column in the final demand part of the table.
- In order to avoid double counting of the external margins, the total of each type of external margin is algebraically added to the cells of the new import column corresponding to the "margin industries."

The new representation no longer includes a row for transferred imports.

All imports consumed by final users are allocated directly to final demand in the row containing "directly allocated imports" (both comparable and noncomparable) in the final demand tables and the capital flow tables for 1963 and 1967. These purchases are balanced by a negative entry in the cell of this row corresponding to the column of net exports. In 1972, comparable imports are combined with domestic goods in each final demand column and balanced by a negative entry in the imports column of final demand. To make 1963 and 1967 CFTs comparable with 1972, aggregate comparable imports for final users have to be allocated among the producing sectors.

Fortunately, the publications of the BEA related to the CFTs for 1963 and 1967 (U.S. Department of Commerce, 1971b, 1975a) provide information on imports of capital goods. We assumed that all imports for 1963 and 1967 were imports of comparable capital goods and distributed all imported commodities like their domestic equivalents, as the BEA did for 1972. The total imports of each capital good were added as a negative entry to the corresponding cell of the new imports column in the final demand tables for 1963 and 1967.

No attempt was made to reallocate the imports absorbed by personal consumption,[1] which in any case accounted for only about 2% of personal consumption expenditures. No adjustments to the final demand tables other than those described above were required for present purposes.

Secondary Products

Even individual establishments frequently produce two or more commodities: the main product is called primary and any others are considered secondary. For many purposes it is desirable to represent secondary products as being produced by the industries to which they are primary; the resulting industries are defined in terms of a single output, facilitating a technological interpretation for the input coefficients. The BEA changed its treatment of secondary products in the 1972 study.

The method used by the BEA in its 1972 study makes an explicit distinction between industry and commodity and involves the USE table which describes the utilization of different commodities by the different industries and the MAKE table which describes the production of different commodities by the different industries. By convention an industry is given the same name as its primary product.

We combined the USE and MAKE tables in order to make an industry-by-industry representation, a choice influenced by availability of employment and capital data on an industry, not commodity or process, basis. A row of the resulting matrix shows the utilization of the mix of commodities produced in the given year by the corresponding industry.

---

1. Full import vectors for the 1963 and 1967 IO tables have been developed in the course of subsequent IEA research (see Leontief and Duchin, 1985).

To reorganize the IO data in this way, we used the pattern of distribution of different commodities as shown in the USE table. The information in the MAKE table makes it possible to attribute a fraction of the total output of each commodity to the industries which actually produce it. This transformation assumes that, when a commodity is produced by several industries, all users buy it in the same proportions from the different producers. These proportions are equal to the share of the different industries in the total production of that commodity.

The algebra of the transformation of a commodity-by-industry to an industry-by-industry classification is as follows:

$$T = WU$$

where T is the industry-by-industry table, W is the coefficient matrix obtained after dividing each cell of the MAKE table by the corresponding column total, and U is the USE table. The same transformation must also be applied to the final demand columns and the CFTs.

The method described above was used for 1972 and 1977, years for which USE and MAKE tables are available. For 1963 and 1967 we reconstructed USE and MAKE tables from published data.

In the studies for 1963 and 1967, the BEA used a "transfer" approach, in which a secondary product is sold by the producing industry to the industry for which it is the primary product. Since this sale is fictitious, the method over-estimates intermediate inputs for the "buying" industry.

Data available from the BEA for these two years show separately the direct allocation (i.e., the real transaction) and the transfer. A table containing only direct allocations is conceptually identical to a USE table. A table containing only transfers is comparable to a MAKE table with empty cells on the main diagonal.

To complete the MAKE table we required, for the main diagonal, the production of each industry's primary commodity. By definition this amount is equal to the total production of that commodity less the amount produced as secondary product by other industries. The total output of a commodity is represented by the corresponding row total of the USE table. The amount produced as secondary product by other industries is the column total of the transfer table. The cells on the main diagonal of the MAKE table were filled using this information, and then the procedure described earlier (for 1972 and 1977) was applied to the 1963 and 1967 IO tables.

Scrap, used, and secondhand goods are treated as secondary products. Since this category of goods is considered a single commodity, every user of scrap appears to use a small amount of the production of every industry producing scrap, used, and secondhand goods.

The number of secondary products identified as such in the later studies is larger than in the earlier ones, and we have not attempted to resolve the discrepancy. In all other respects, the methodology described above allows us to prepare the input-output tables for 1963, 1967, 1972, and 1977, such that each treats secondary products in the same way.

Eating and Drinking Places

In this section we describe the methods used to resolve the inconsistencies created by the lack of an Eating and Drinking Places (E&D) sector in the 1963 and 1967 IO tables. Prior to 1972 E&D (IEA #78, BEA #74) was included in Retail Trade as a margin sector. This meant that its input structure did not include the purchase of food, beverages, and other materials but only the margin costs of providing a service (electricity, containers, etc.). Since 1972 it is treated as a separate, productive sector that transforms the product it sells.

We have created an E&D row and column and removed E&D activities from other sectors for 1963 and 1967, using the following information:

- Structure of E&D (column and row) in the BEA 1972 table.
- Gross output of E&D in 1963 and 1967 (provided by BLS).
- Industrial composition of Personal Consumption Expenditure by PCE category, in producers' and purchasers' prices ("bridge tables") (U.S. Department of Commerce, 1971a, 1974b).

The BEA publishes tables of purchases of meals and beverages for personal consumption, shown for 1967 in Table B.3. These purchases correspond exactly to personal consumption of E&D, which accounts for over three-fourths of E&D output and provides the basis for our E&D column.

While Wholesale Trade and Retail Trade are combined in Table B.3, they need to be distinguished for the E&D column since the first is a cost (i.e., an input) and the second is now a part of the product.

The 1967 IO study provides the trade margins for the aggregate deliveries of the sectors identified in Table B.3; these margins are shown in Table B.4. In constructing the E&D column we assume that

TABLE B.3. Purchases of Meals and Beverages Out of Personal Consumption Expenditures in 1967 (Millions of 1967 Dollars)

Producing sector (BEA codes)	Producers' prices	Transportation	Trade margin	Purchasers' prices
1 Livestock and Livestock Products	$ 126	$ 9	$ 204	$ 339
2 Other Agricultural Products	361	52	628	1,042
3 Forestry and Fishery Products	271	53	392	716
14 Food and Kindred Products	8,379	186	13,230	21,795
27 Chemicals and Selected Chemical Products	8	0	7	15
69 Wholesale Trade	541	0	0	541
80 Noncomparable Imports	6	1	12	19
Total	9,692	302	14,473	24,467

Source: U.S. Department of Commerce (1974b).

149

TABLE B.4.   Distribution of Retail and Wholesale Trade Among Sectors Supplying Purchased Meals and Beverages to Personal Consumption in 1967 (Millions of 1967 Dollars)

	Producing sector (BEA code)	Direct allocation	Retail trade	Wholesale trade	Wholesale trade/ direct allocation
1	Livestock and Livestock Products	$ 18,112	$ 4,264	$ 1,581	.087
2	Other Agricultural Products	37,562	24,927	6,136	.163
3	Factory and Fishery Products	4,486	4,002	960	.214
14	Food and Kindred Products	609,746	252,071	79,858	.131
27	Chemicals and Selected Chemical Products	5,046	2,135	321	.064

Source: U.S. Department of Commerce (tape, 1974a).

Wholesale Trade is the same proportion of direct allocation as it is for the total sales of the corresponding sector.

Finally, total E&D output is available for 1963 and 1967 (U.S. Department of Labor, 1982a). For 1967 it was $34,312 million or $75,138 million in 1979 prices (the value unit for the IEA database).

The E&D column can now be constructed. First, the total value of E&D output at purchasers' price is distributed between the value of the product and transportation and trade margins according to the proportions given in the last row of Table B.3; this is shown explicitly in the last row of Table B.5. Then the product is distributed among the seven producing sectors in the same proportions as in the first column of Table B.3; this is shown in the first column of Table B.5. The wholesale component of the trade margin is estimated by applying the ratios in the last column of Table B.4 to the direct allocation in the first column of Table B.5. This produces an estimate of the retail trade margin as the difference between the total trade margin and the total wholesale margin. The retail trade portion is then multiplied by the input coefficient vector of the retail trade sector, and these flows are treated as additional inputs to E&D. The prices are now inflated to 1979 prices and easily assembled into a column of input coefficients.

The 1963 and 1967 E&D coefficient columns constructed in this way were roughly comparable with the one for 1972, except for Crude Petroleum and Natural Gas (IEA #8). This sector provided virtually no input into E&D in 1972, while our construction resulted in a substantial flow for 1963 and 1967 which we set to zero in the absence of a substantive explanation for a large input in the earlier years.

TABLE B.5. Input Structure of Eating and Drinking Places in 1967 (Millions of 1967 Dollars)

Producing sector (BEA codes)	Producers' prices	Transportation margin	Retail trade margin	Wholesale trade margin	Purchasers' prices
1 Livestock and Livestock Products	$ 177			$ 15	
2 Other Agricultural Products	506			83	
3 Forestry and Fishery Products	380			81	
14 Food and Kindred Products	11,750			1,539	
27 Chemicals and Selected Chemical Products	11			1	
69 Wholesale Trade	759			—	
80 Noncomparable Imports	8			—	
Total	13,592	423	(18,578)	(1,719)	34,312

20,297

The E&D sector is known to sell about three-fourths of its output to personal consumption. In the absence of additional information, the E&D rows were constructed by allocating the remaining 25% of its output according to the 1972 distribution.

The input structures of other sectors were adjusted to be consistent with this treatment of E&D. No longer do they purchase food from the foodstuff-producing sectors and a margin from Retail Trade; this now comes as a package from E&D. Reductions in the affected inputs were made for all purchasing sectors using the same information needed to construct the E&D column.

Deflation

In order to represent all values in base year 1979 prices, the deflators prepared by the Office of Economic Growth of the BLS were selected for the following reasons:

- They are deflators of gross sectoral output (rather than value added deflators used in the National Accounts).
- They are industry deflators and take into account the product mix of the individual sector and its change over time.
- The classification follows closely the BEA IO classification and is available at a high level of disaggregation (155 sectors).

To take full advantage of the detail of the BLS deflators, the final demand, transactions, and capital flow tables were deflated at this level and then aggregated to the IEA 85-sector classification; this step involved the reconciliation of classification schemes. 1979 was chosen as the base year because it was the latest year for which detailed price data were available when this work was done.

While the BLS series shows almost no price change in Electronic Computing and Related Equipment (IEA #50) over the period 1963–1977, the business and technical literature suggests that the price has in fact been declining at least 10% a year on the average. A similar observation holds for Semiconductors and Related Devices (IEA #58). The BLS deflators were replaced by a 10% per year decline in price for both sectors. While other official deflators may also over-estimate price increases because of a conservative assessment of changes in the nature or quality of the output, these are the most important cases for the purposes of this study.

A separate issue arises in the case of the so-called service sectors, in which the official total output deflators are in many cases based (inappropriately) on the changing cost of labor inputs. For this study, we have defined "physical" measures of output for private and public education, IEA #83 and #89, whose output we represent in millions of student-years, and for Instructional Television (ITV) and Computer-Based Instruction (CBI), IEA #87 and #88, whose output is measured in terms of hours of electronic courseware.

Coefficient Matrices 1963–1977

Interindustry Transactions (A Matrix)

After the data had been standardized, deflated, and aggregated to the IEA 85-sector classification as described above, the parts of the IO tables for 1963, 1967, 1972, and 1977 containing the interindustry flows were organized into an A matrix of technical coefficients for each of these benchmark years. Each technical coefficient is obtained by dividing an entry of the flow table by the corresponding row total. Thus the element in the ith row and j^{th} column of an A matrix is computed as the total amount of output of sector i consumed by sector j, divided by the total output of sector j in the corresponding time period (measured in 1979 prices or in physical units). For years between benchmark years, each coefficient was linearly interpolated.

Replacement of Fixed Nonresidential Capital (R Matrix)

In the dynamic IEA model replacement of existing capital and investment for expansion are treated separately. While a sector's planned increases in the productive capacity provided by its stock of physical capital are determined by comparing projected future capacity requirements with capacity already in place, investment to replace fixed assets is assumed to depend upon the current level of sectoral activity.[2] In either case the *composition* of investment will be dictated essentially by technical requirements. This section describes the methodology for allocating past gross investment between replacement and

---

2. Investment also takes place for technological modernization in the absence of growth: capital may replace noncapital inputs or obsolescent capital. This issue arises, for example, in the case of robots (Chapter 2).

expansion and for computing the coefficients of the replacement matrix, R. The ith element of the jth column of R specifies the amount of output of sector i purchased by sector j to maintain its productive capacity during a particular time period.

In the absence of systematic, direct observation of the fixed capital in each industry, official government series on capital stocks use a "perpetual inventory" approach to record the accumulation of new capital and the discarding of existing assets using an initial observation of stocks, subsequent data on gross investment, and assumptions about the lifetimes of different capital goods. Within this framework, replacement investment is that which compensates for the retirement of fixed assets. For those sectors whose capital stock is contracting, scrapping of fixed assets exceeds replacement, and we have attempted to represent the amount of replacement that actually takes place.

The BLS publishes annual data on capital stock, investment, and retirement of equipment and structures by industry, computed in a perpetual-inventory framework, for the years from 1947 to 1974 (U.S. Department of Labor, 1979).[3] These data do not specify the physical composition of the stocks or flows. We have relied for the latter information on the BEA capital flow tables for 1963, 1967, and 1972, which describe the deliveries in a given year of over 600 capital goods to each sector of the economy in the 2-digit BEA classification (i.e., 77 capital-using sectors). These tables were standardized, deflated, and aggregated as described earlier. Column totals measure each industry's gross investment, and column proportions show the corresponding composition. Sectoral gross investment data reported by the BLS and those prepared by BEA do not always rely on the same sources and are not identical. We adopted the BEA series to maintain as much consistency as possible with the rest of the input-output data.

The replacement flow matrices are computed in the following way. The BLS ratio of discards to gross investment is multiplied by the BEA estimate of gross investment, resulting in the level of replacement investment of the given sector in a particular year. The composition of this replacement investment is assumed to be the same as that of the corresponding sector's gross investment as reported in the CFT. Each sector's replacement of equipment and of structures (the latter assumed to be produced exclusively by the construction sector) is computed separately and takes into account the relatively slower rate of

---

3. The Bureau of Industrial Economics in the U.S. Department of Commerce recently made available a new set of data on capital stocks by industry which has not been incorporated in the present study.

replacement of structures. Finally, the technical coefficients of the R matrix are computed by dividing these flows of replacement capital by the total output of the using sector. This representation of replacement reflects the assumption that a sector will replace only the portion of its stock required for current production.

Since the CFTs exist only for 1963, 1967, and 1972, R matrices can be directly computed only for these years. For the years in between, each coefficient was linearly interpolated. The 1972 R matrix was repeated for each year through 1977, with a few exceptions which are noted in Chapter 2.

Expansion of Fixed Nonresidential Capital (B Matrix)

The jth column of the expansion matrix, B, measures the stock of each type of capital good required to increase the capacity of sector j by one unit. The stock of each kind of capital good is measured in the same unit as the output of the sector that produces it. In the present case, this unit is a 1979 dollar's worth.

Especially in capital-intensive sectors, very detailed plans are on the drawing boards of engineers years before a capital project is actually realized. Investigators at the Battelle Memorial Institute have made use of this type of information to produce expansion matrices like those required for our database (Fisher and Chilton, 1971). While it proved impractical to use the Battelle matrices due to the impossibility of assuring consistency between the conventions used in constructing these tables and those employed in assembling the rest of our database, this so-called *ex ante* method for constructing the B matrix seems promising for future work. The present study relied on the accounting information in the government data series.

While data are available on annual sectoral output and net investment (the latter series resulting from the data work described in the preceding section of this chapter), it was not possible to deduce a technologically meaningful relationship between the two without taking into account other factors, such as sectoral rates of capacity utilization.

Instead of deducing stock requirement from the capital flow data, we chose instead to use the sectoral capital-to-output ratio to govern the total amount of capital required for a unit expansion in capacity. It is true that capital-to-output ratios measure the average capital requirement, rather than incorporating the most advanced techniques that are typically used by new facilities and that are conceptually required by our representation. Until better data are available, we can observe that using the average in place of the "best technology" ratio does not introduce a systematic over- or under-statement of net investment, since the average and, therefore, best technology ratio does not appear to be monotonic but depends upon specific technological events (see, for example, Duchin, 1984).

The B matrices for 1963, 1967, and 1972 were prepared in the following way. Sectoral capital stock estimates for the benchmark years in 1972 prices, available in U.S. Department of Labor (1979), were inflated to 1979 prices using the NIPA price index for nonresidential fixed investment (U.S. Department of Commerce, 1982). These measures of the total capital stock held by each sector were divided by corresponding sectoral outputs, resulting in sectoral capital-to-output ratios. Since the industrial classification of the capital stock series is less detailed than the IEA classification, a single capital-to-output ratio was in several instances used for more than one sector.[4] (While the specification of the model calls for full-capacity output in the denominator of the capital-to-output ratios, we did not make this adjustment for the present study.)

The vectors of capital-to-ouput ratios for a given year, measuring total stocks required to produce a unit of output, are by definition the column totals of the corresponding B matrix. Expansion capital was assumed to have the same product composition as gross investment, so the column totals were distributed over capital-producing sectors in the same proportions as in the columns of the capital flow tables for the corresponding years. The coefficients of the B matrices were computed in this way, and then interpolated between benchmark years and projected to 1977 in the same way as that described in the last section for the R matrix.

The B matrix is subsequently decomposed into B^θ, $\theta = 1,2,3$, according to the lag between the delivery of a capital item and its effective use in production.

Initial Conditions and Control Totals

The IEA model requires estimates of sectoral capacity for the initial year and projections of future capacity (based on estimated sectoral expansion plans) for the next five years (as discussed in Appendix A).

---

4. The industrial classification of the capital stock series follows the 2-digit IO classification with two exceptions: the four agricultural sectors (BEA #1–4) are aggregated together, as are New and Maintenance Construction (BEA #11 and 12).

Ceilings on the growth of capacity and lags also need to be specified. In addition, during the development of the model it was necessary to prepare "control totals" for sectoral outputs and investment to check the values produced by the model. This section describes the preparation of data for initial conditions and controls.

TABLE B.6.   Capacity Utilization by Sector in 1963

Sector		Capacity[a] utilization
5,6	Metal Mining	.81
7	Coal Mining	.82
8	Crude Petroleum and Natural Gas	.91
9,10	Stone and Earth Minerals Mining	.88
11	Construction	.89
12	Ordnance and Accessories	.68
13	Food and Kindred Products	.90
14	Tobacco Manufacturers	.96
15,16	Textiles	.84
17,18	Apparel and Miscellaneous Fabricated Textiles	.94
19,20	Lumber and Wood Products	.90
21,22	Furniture and Fixtures	.87
23,24	Paper and Allied Products	.85
25	Printing and Publishing	.87
26–29	Chemicals, Plastics, Drugs, and Paints	.79
30	Petroleum Refining and Allied Industries	.93
31	Rubber and Miscellaneous Plastics Products	.78
32,33	Leather Products	.93
34,35	Glass, Stone, and Clay Products	.92
36	Primary Iron and Steel Manufacturing	.80
37	Primary Nonferrous Metals Manufacturing	.80
38–41	Fabricated Metals	.83
42–52	Machinery, except Electrical	.72
53–60	Electrical Machinery	.82
61	Motor Vehicles and Equipment	.85
62	Aircraft and Parts	.68
64,65	Instruments	.83
66	Miscellaneous Manufacturing	.85
67	Transportation and Warehousing	.85
70	Electric, Gas, Water, and Sanitary Services	.94
71,72	Trade	.94
76	Hotel, Personal, and Repair Services, except Auto	.66
86	Robotics	—
	All other sectors	1.00

Source: U.S. Department of Commerce (1975b).

[a]Defined as proportion of "preferred" rates of utilization as in the source.

TABLE B.7.   Sectoral Lags

Code	Sector	Years
11	Construction	3
12	Ordnance and Accessories	2
36	Primary Iron and Steel Manufacturing	2
37	Primary Nonferrous Metals Manufacturing	2
39	Heating, Plumbing, and Structural Metal Products	2
40	Screw Machine Products and Stamping	2
41	Other Fabricated Metal Products	2
42	Engines and Turbines	2
46	Metalworking Machinery and Equipment	2
47	Special Industry Machinery and Equipment	2
48	General Industrial Machinery and Equipment	2
49	Miscellaneous Machinery Except Electrical	2
50	Electronic Computing and Related Equipment	2 (1)[a]
52	Service Industry Machines	2
53	Electric Industrial Equipment and Apparatus	2
60	Miscellaneous Electrical Machinery and Supplies	2
64	Scientific and Controlling Instruments	2
65	Optical, Ophthalmical, and Photographic Equipment	2
	All other capital-producing sectors	1

[a]The lag for IEA #50, Electronic Computing and Related Equipment, is 2 from 1963 to 1969, and 1 thereafter.

When a sector's capital stock is being fully utilized, its productive capacity is equal to its output. Given its output and an estimated rate of capacity utilization, the capacity can be computed. Sectoral capacities for 1963 were derived in this fashion from utilization rates published by BEA (U.S. Department of Commerce, 1975b), using a classification scheme very close to ours.[5] When the BEA sectors were more aggregated than the IEA classification, we used the same rate for each part of the larger sector. For those sectors not explicitly reported (exclusively service sectors), we followed the source document in assuming 100% capacity utilization. The ratios used in the model are given in Table B.6.

We know of no systematic empirical work on the lag, by item of physical capital, between the time it is delivered and when it becomes productive. In all the computations carried out for this report, we have assumed a maximum lag $\tau = 3$ in order to permit a crude distinction among plant, major equipment, and capital items that are likely to be

5. This source defines these rates as "actual utilization rates as a percent of preferred utilization rates."

put into production shortly after delivery. Table B.7 shows the lags, τ_i, of from 1 to 3 periods assigned to the different capital-producing sectors. They are very rough estimates and in future work should be based on empirical investigation.

The sectoral ceilings on annual anticipated rates of real growth of output, δ_i, which are used in the determination of future capacity (but do not directly constrain the sector's future growth), are shown in Table B.8. For most sectors that ceiling is assumed to be 5%, potentially limiting expansion investment so that at full-capacity utilization, real output capacity four periods ahead will be no more than 21.6% higher than output in the current period. (The model permits more than "full" utilization of capacity, however.) As shown in the table, 12 sectors were assumed to operate with higher limits on anticipated growth for purposes of capital planning.

Output vectors for benchmark years were produced by standardizing, deflating, and aggregating the IO transaction flow tables (see "Coefficient Matrices 1963–1977," in this appendix) and these vectors were linearly interpolated for the years in between. These data were used both to estimate capacity through 1964–1968 and as controls to check the performance of the model and signal potential problems.

Controls were also prepared for fixed nonresidential replacement and expansion investment. These numbers were computed from a

TABLE B.8. Maximum Annual Anticipated Growth Rates for Projection of Future Capacity Requirements

Code	Sector	Real rate of growth
50	Electronic Computing and Related Equipment	20% (15,12)[a]
51	Office equipment, except IEA #50	15
57	Electron Tubes	10
58	Semiconductors and Related Devices	15
59	Other Electronic Components, nec	15
77	Business Services	10
81	Hospitals	7
82	Health Services, excluding Hospitals	7
83	Educational Services	7
86	Robotics	15
87	Instructional TV	20
88	Computer-Based Instruction	20
	All other	5

[a]The maximum rate for IEA #50, Electronic Computing and Related Equipment, is 20% from 1963 to 1969, 15% from 1970 to 1979, and 12% thereafter.

TABLE B.9. IEA Occupational Classification and Corresponding BLS Codes

IEA code	Description of occupation	BLS code[a]
Professionals		
1	Electrical Engineers	10020200
2	Industrial Engineers	10020250
3	Mechanical Engineers	10020300
4	Other Engineers	1002 (except 10020200, 10020250, 10020300)
5	Natural Scientists	1004, 1006
6	Computer Programmers	10160050
7	Computer Systems Analysts	10160100
8	Other Computer Specialists	10160150
9	Personnel and Labor Relations Workers	10240650
10	Physicians and Surgeons	10100300
11	Registered Nurses	10100400
12	Other Medical Professionals	1010 (except 10100300, 10100400)
13	Health Technologists, Technicians	1012000
14	Teachers	10200000
15	Drafters	10080150
16	Other Professional, Technical	1014, 1018, 1022, 1024 (except 10240650)
Managers		1008 (except 10080150)
17	Managers, Officials, Proprietors	20000000
Sales Workers		
18	Sales Workers	30000000
Clerical Workers		
19	Stenographers, Typists, Secretaries	40020000
20	Office Machine Operators	40040000
21	Bank Tellers	40060050
22	Telephone Operators	40061550
23	Cashiers	40060200
24	Other Clerical	4006 (except 40060050, 40061550, 40060200)
Craftsmen		
25	Carpenters	50020050
26	Electricians	50020350
27	Plumbers and Pipefitters	50020800
28	Other Construction Craft Workers	5002 (except 50020050, 50020350, 50020800)
29	Foreman, nec	50040000
30	Machinists	50060300
31	Tool and Die Makers	50060750

TABLE B.9 *(cont'd)*. IEA Occupational Classification and Corresponding BLS Codes

IEA code	Description of occupation	BLS code[a]
Professionals		
32	Other Metal Working Craft Workers	5006 (except 50060300, 50060750)
33	Mechanics, Repairers	50080000
34	Printing Trade Craft Workers	50100000
35	Transportation, Public Utilities Crafts, Other Craft Workers	50120000
36	Bakers	50140500
37	Crane, Derrick and Hoist Operators	50140200
38	Other Craft Workers	5014 (except 50140050, 50140200)
Operatives		
39	Assemblers	61080100
40	Checkers, Examiners, Inspectors	61060050
41	Packers and Wrappers	61060200
42	Painters	61081050
43	Welders and Flame Cutters	61020500
44	Delivery and Route Workers	62000200
45	Truck Drivers	62000550
46	Other Operatives	6000 (except 61080100, 61060050, 61060200, 61081050, 6102, 62000200, 62000550)
47	Robot Technicians[b]	—
Service Workers		
48	Janitors and Sextons	70020150
49	Protective Service Workers	70100000
50	Food Service Workers	70040050, 70040150, 70040250, 70040300
51	Other Service Workers	7000 (except 70120000, 70020150, 70100000, 70040050, 70040150, 70040250, 70040300)
Laborers		
52	Laborers	8000
Farmers and Farm Workers		
53	Farmers and Farm Workers	9000

[a]Unpublished BLS classification scheme (U.S. Department of Labor, 1981).

[b]In aggregate occupational classification schemes Robot Technicians, IEA #47, are included as Craftsmen.

recent BEA publication (U.S. Dept. of Commerce, 1982) which provides annual gross fixed nonresidential investment through 1979 in current and constant 1972 dollars, separately for equipment and structures, as well as discards of fixed capital. Separate deflators for equipment and structures were computed to convert the series to 1979 prices.

Employment Data

The final requirement of the IEA model was for data on the use of labor by occupation per unit of each sector's output. The principal sources of information are the occupation-by-industry matrices prepared by the BLS for 1960, 1970, and 1978 (from U.S. Department of Labor, 1973, 1981).

The occupation-by-industry matrix for 1960 is based on the 1960 Census of Population and includes 186 occupations and 157 industries. The matrix for 1970 is based on the 1970 census, while that for 1978 is an update incorporating data from various surveys. These last two matrices include 425 occupations and 260 industries. Neither the sectoral nor the occupational classification scheme is compatible with that of the 1960 matrix.

For this study we used a 53-occupation classification scheme, given in Table B.9. At this level of aggregation, the BLS employment categories for 1960 and later years were comparable with only a few discrepancies that were resolved using further detail from the 1960 Census of Population.

To ensure compatibility with the IEA sectoral classification, we attempted to match sector definitions of the three BLS employment matrices to the IEA 85-sector classification at the level of the component SIC codes. When the BLS sector included several IEA sectors, the corresponding employment levels were decomposed according to sectoral outputs assuming the same occupational structure for each subsector. Once the classificational discrepancies were reconciled, the employment data took the form of three flow matrices of 53 occupations by 85 sectors for 1960, 1970, and 1978.[6] The row totals of these matrices show private-sector employment by occupation, and the column totals correspond to private-sector employment by sector of the economy.

---

6. In fact, a fourth matrix was prepared based on BLS projections for 1990. It is used in this study only for purposes of comparison with IEA projections (in Chapter 1).

The BEA has published aggregate employment by IO sector, using the definitions and conventions of their IO studies for 1967 and 1972 (U.S. Department of Commerce, 1978, 1981b). Discrepancies for some sectors between these data and the column totals of the BLS matrices were resolved by augmenting the BEA totals by estimates of the number of self-employed by sector from other sources. BLS matrices were used to determine the occupational composition of employment for each sector. BEA sectoral employment is consistent with the NIPA employment series which, while more aggregated in their sectoral classification, were available for 1963 and 1977 as well as 1967 and 1972 (U.S. Department of Commerce, 1981a, 1982). The NIPA data for 1963 and 1972 were disaggregated to 85 sectors using proportions from the 1967 and 1972 BEA employment studies, respectively, when necessary.

The three matrices of occupational proportions (for 1960, 1970, and 1978) were interpolated linearly to produce four matrices for the benchmark years (1963, 1967, 1972, and 1977). The four corresponding vectors of total employment by sector were divided, element by element, by total sectoral output (in 1979 prices) in the given year, resulting in sectoral labor-to-output ratios. Finally these ratios were distributed among occupations according to the matrices of occupational proportions. The final outcome was a set of four matrices for the years 1963, 1967, 1972, and 1977 of labor-to-output ratios by occupation and by sector.

Coefficient Matrices 1978–1980

Each scenario for which data have been developed in Chapters 2 through 6 of this volume specifies A, R, B, and L coefficient matrices for 1990 and 2000. The most recent government IO data are for 1977, and these were in most cases simply repeated for 1978, 1979, and 1980 with exceptions for newly emerging sectors. The sectors producing electronic educational courseware (IEA #87 and 88) appear in 1980, and the robotics sector (IEA #86) begins production in 1977. Annual matrices are produced by interpolation for 1981–89 and 1991–99.

REFERENCES

Duchin, F. 1984. Automation and its impacts on employment. In *American Jobs and the Changing Industrial Base*, eds. E. Collins and L. Tanner. Cambridge, Mass.: Ballinger Publishing Co.

Fisher, W. Halder, and Cecil H. Chilton. 1971. *Final Report on an Ex Ante Capital Matrix for the United States, 1970-1975 to Scientific American.* Columbus, Ohio: Battelle Memorial Institute.

Leontief, W., and F. Duchin, principal investigators. Automation, the changing pattern of U.S. exports and imports, and their implications for employment. Prepared for National Science Foundation, PRA 83-11407 (March 1985).

U.S. Department of Commerce. Bureau of Economic Analysis. *Input-Output Structure of the U.S. Economy: 1963.* 3 vols. Washington, D.C. (1969).

————. Personal consumption expenditure in the 1963 input-output study. *Survey of Current Business.* Washington, D.C. (January 1971a).

————. *Notes on Methods and Sources Used in Preparing the 1963 Capital Flow Tables.* Washington, D.C. (November 1971b).

————. *Input-Output Structure of the U.S. Economy: 1967.* 3 vols. and magnetic tape. Washington, D.C. (1974)a.

————. The input-output structure of the U.S. economy: 1967. *Survey of Current Business.* Washington, D.C. (February 1974b).

————. *Interindustry Transactions in New Structures and Equipment, 1963 and 1967.* 2 vols. Washington, D.C. (1975)a.

————. *A Study of Fixed Capital Requirements of the U.S. Business Economy, 1971–1980.* Washington, D.C. (December 1975b).

————. *Employment and Employee Compensation in the 1967 Input-Output Study.* BEA Staff Paper no. 31. Washington, D.C. (February 1978).

————. *The Detailed Input-Output Structure of the U.S. Economy: 1972.* 2 vols. Washington, D.C. (1979).

————. *New Structures and Equipment by Using Industry, 1972: Detailed Estimates and Methodology.* Washington, D.C. (1980).

————. *The National Income and Product Accounts of the United States, 1929–76 Statistical Tables.* Washington, D.C. (September 1981a).

————. *Employment and Employee Compensation in the 1972 Input-Output Study.* BEA Staff Paper no. 38. Washington, D.C. (October 1981b).

————. Revised estimates of the national income and product accounts. *Survey of Current Business.* 63: no. 7. Washington, D.C. (July 1982).

U.S. Department of Labor. Bureau of Labor Statistics. *Tomorrow's Manpower Needs.* 4 vols., Bulletin no. 1737. Washington, D.C. (1973).

————. *Capital Stock Estimates for Input Output Industries: Methods and Data.* Bulletin 2034. Washington, D.C. (1979).

————. *The National Industry-Occupation Employment Matrix, 1970, 1978, and Projected 1990.* Bulletin 2086. 2 vols. Washington, D.C. (1981).

————. *Time Series Data for Input-Output Industries: Output, Price, and Employment.* Unpublished update on computer tape DATA, SIC 72, received October 1982a.

————. Unpublished BLS 1977 current dollar MAKE and USE tables and final demands, received October 1982b.

U.S. Executive Office of the President. Office of Management and Budget. *Standard Industrial Classification Manual,* Washington, D.C. (1957, 1967, 1972).

Index